No More Secrets and Lies

A MJ Lange Mystery

Cindy Kludt

No More Secrets and Lies

A MJ Lange Mystery

For more information, email kludt@mac.com

ISBN: 979-8-89109-040-8 - paperback

ISBN: 979-8-89109-041-5- ebook

Get Your Free Gift!

Attention all crime drama and psychological thriller fans!

I am excited to share with you a glimpse into the backstory of wounded healer, psychologist, MJ Lange.

What happened to her as a teenager that led to her struggles with alcoholism and fueled her desire to save and help people, even if it meant putting herself in perilous situations while solving the mysteries?

If you love to understand the inner psychological working of the mind, this prequel will satisfy that need.

You can read the prequel of the MJ Lange mystery series by visiting:

https://cindykludtauthor.com/free-prequel

With love to Andy and Stephanie

Table of Contents

Chapter 1

It had been six months since I killed a man.

The construction noise woke me early, or early to me, since I hadn't stopped flailing around in bed until 5 a.m. when I finally got to sleep. It seemed like I had just gotten to sleep when the banging started.

I looked at my watch which read 9 a.m. and I was mortified, since I always tried to be up by six or seven. Anything past 8 a.m. feels to me like the day has already been wasted.

Kicking the covers off, I jumped out of bed and ran to use the bathroom before going into the kitchen to partake of the strong coffee I knew Aunt Carrie had brewed earlier. I was a little embarrassed that I had wasted so much of the day.

"You up?" I heard her shout. She has a loud voice, which I appreciate since I have a 50% hearing loss.

Her voice is the one voice I can hear clearly without my hearing aids. It's loud and filled with joy. I've never seen her angry and I've never seen her talk badly to anyone or about anyone.

This didn't mean she wasn't very assertive when she needed to be. Some people were a bit intimidated by her loudness, but once they got to know her, they realized she was like a large mama bear, fiercely protective to all those she loved.

I had come to live with Aunt Carrie soon after the incident. She had jumped at the opportunity to buy the house next door to mine and had invited me to live with her so I could supervise the new construction that was needed on my house after the fire. "Someone has to look after you, MJ," she had said. "You're clearly not eating. Look at you, you're nothing but skin and bones."

Now I shouted back to her that I was indeed up and would be out in a minute. I was quick; I slept in my sweats, so didn't need time to get dressed.

Aunt Carrie was sitting at the kitchen table with a cup of her strong coffee in front of her and a plate of her to-die-for homemade cinnamon rolls. I could see that she had already eaten two of them and was sure she'd join me with another.

She was just a little taller than my five foot three inches, but carried a hefty weight, giving her that round jolly look. She wore short fringe bangs similar to Mamie Eisenhower's, and along with her shapeless house dress, she looked like she just stepped out of a 1950s catalog. Sitting in her 50s kitchen added to the look, and it made me feel safe, like I was living in a "Father Knows Best" sitcom.

I came up behind her and gave her a hug from the back as I forced a cheery good morning, and then went to pour myself a cup of her strong and somewhat bitter coffee. Since she added a lot of cream and sugar to her coffee, she couldn't taste the bitterness and I didn't complain about it. It wasn't right for me to dictate how she did things in her own home, when I was just a guest. Besides, I was getting used to the bitterness and now I actually rather liked the jolt I was getting from it.

"What's on your agenda for today?"

I hesitated because I was fearful that she would start nagging me, like my best friend Franny, about getting back to work.

"The reason I ask is because I need a little advice."

"Oh?" I raised my eyebrows in a question.

"It's about April."

April was her daughter and lived in a more gritty part of Venice with her three year old daughter Joey, and her boyfriend Alex, Joey's father.

Aunt Carrie had hinted in the past about trouble between April and Alex, but being someone who didn't like to gossip or speak ill about anyone, she never told me the entire story of what was wrong.

I was close to Aunt Carrie, so I found it a bit odd that I had only met April and her daughter once, and had never met Alex. I often enquired about them but Aunt Carrie usually just said that they had a busy life and she didn't want to interfere. I knew there was something more because I could often see the hurt in her eyes, all the while coming to April's defense.

"Okay, what wise advice do you need from your humble servant?"

I was kidding and assumed she would kid me back or laugh. Instead, she sat across from me and looked at me with a pained expression.

"Aunt Carrie, what's wrong?"

"Oh, I guess I'm just being silly, but I'm worried about April and Joey."

"Did something happen?"

"No, nothing out of the ordinary. It's just that April called me from a strange number the other day and told me that she was finally kicking Alex out."

"Oh dear, did she say why? Are they having trouble?"

"I've never been a fan of Alex, if you must know. We've never gotten along. That's why I don't get to see April and Joey very much. He keeps them isolated and he's very demanding of April's time. Joey always seems frightened whenever I've seen her around her dad. I'm not sure what to think."

My professional mind, not to mention my personal experience, went on alert and I immediately thought, *spousal abuse*. Keeping his partner isolated and being demanding and controlling were some of the warning signs for abuse. I didn't want to scare Aunt Carrie, so I just listened and gave her a nod indicating she should go on.

"It sounded like she was calling from a place of business because there was a lot of noise in the background."

She reached for another cinnamon roll and put it on her plate, indicating that I should help myself. But she remained silent.

"Aunt Carrie, are you worried about April? Have you seen or heard something that worries you?"

She flipped her hand as if shooing a fly away and said with a concerned smile, "Nothing bad happened that I know of, but April has become very secretive since the birth of Joey. She's holding something back. We no longer have that close relationship we once had. I think it has to do with Alex. I don't like him one bit."

"Did you ask her what was going on?"

"No, I never got the chance, she hung up quickly, like someone was there and she had to go.

I didn't like the sound of it. If Alex really was physically abusive, and if April had just kicked him out, then the time right now was very dangerous. It would be the time the abuser could get the angriest and try to keep his control over his partner, often with physical intimidation.

"Look," I cautiously started, "why don't you call April, or go over and see her and suggest she come stay with you for a while. That way she'll be safe and the two of you can reconnect and maybe come up with a plan for how she'll disengage with Alex. I'd be glad to help the two of you, not as a psychologist, but as a friend."

I could see the relief in her face as she reached for another cinnamon roll saying, "Thank you, MJ, I'll do it. Now, eat your cinnamon roll before I eat them all."

Laughing, I took another big bite and then followed it with a sip of the bitter coffee. The taste of the sweet, followed by the bitter and the conversation about someone else's problems took my mind off of the revolving mantra in my mind for the last six months: *I killed a man.*

Chapter 2

I had puttered around for a while after pouring myself another cup of bitter coffee and watched as Aunt Carrie went out the back door to look after her garden. Since it was November, there had been no more vegetables. That part of the garden was dry and looked wilted and dead. But Aunt Carrie had a green thumb and she maintained a beautiful flower garden, even in the winter months. I have never been able to make anything grow, and I had no idea what kinds of flowers she grew. They were a beautiful, colorful lot, and I enjoyed sitting on the patio and taking it all in.

Outside, I sat on a comfy patio chair and sipped my coffee. It was a beautiful warm day and I turned my face up toward the sun. It had felt good helping Aunt Carrie with her 'problem' and I realized that it was indeed time for me to go back to work. Franny was right, it was time for me to do what I do best: help people, or at least try my best to help them.

I sat for a while longer watching Aunt Carrie pull weeds in her slow and methodical manner and I felt safe again, for the first time in six months.

Standing, I yelled out to her, "Aunt Carrie, I'm going to go over to my office for a bit. I'll see you later. Don't make lunch for me."

As I walked through the gate that separated our two properties, I had to be careful as I trudged through my backyard. It was dirty and messy with debris from the beginning of the construction and I had to be careful of nails and other materials that might be sticking out for me to trip over.

There was no one working on my house as I gazed at the demolition, seeing some of the charred remains from the fire. Looking at it made me uncomfortable. I realized that having to look at the evidence of that fire triggered a stress reaction inside of me and I was avoiding spending any time at the house, or in the back garage office. I made a mental note to tell the contractor to please get rid of the fire evidence as soon as possible.

I turned away from the chaos of the construction site and started up the outside stairs to reach my office. Franny had loaned me the money to remodel the apartment above the garage into an office space for me. It had been finished for a few months, but I hadn't really used it, although I had bought a few items like a desk, a sofa-bed, and a couple of chairs for my clients and me. It was all new and smelled like fresh paint.

A small kitchenette was semi-hidden on the far wall, next to the small bathroom, and there were windows across the entire office looking out over my house and beyond. The house was only one level but from my office above the garage, I could see the ocean and Venice Beach. I loved the space. The ocean glistened in the sun and my mood jumped up a notch.

I made a silent apology to my inner traumatic hurt self, knowing that I had been licking my wounds these past 6 months instead of living my life. I had just started to come alive again after my husband Gideon had died. Then all hell broke loose when my friend Joe was murdered by Mike Rimichi, who disguised himself as Detective Slatter. The murder of Joe and the betrayal of a man I thought was a police detective caused me considerable anxiety and fear. I was determined to rise up from this trauma and live my full life.

I stood gazing out the window at the ocean for a while, and then looked around my office. There was an excitement stirring inside me and I couldn't wait to start decorating. I'm not very good at it, but I liked the idea of starting all over and picking out things that I would like. Not things I should like, or I should get, but what I would actually enjoy.

I ran down the stairs, picked my way back to Aunt Carrie's house and told her I was going shopping, then jumped into the shower and got ready. Since I didn't have much money, I'd start somewhere like Target, or drive around to see if there were any garage sales going on. I hummed in the shower and felt really good about my decision to start work again. I had been moping around enough. It was time for me to take action. I refused to allow the trauma of what happened to me keep me down.

Yup, I was back in the saddle. No one was going to ever keep me from living my life again. My trauma therapist was going to be thrilled with my actions.

***

I spent most of my shopping time just looking around, not wanting to hurry into any purchases that would make me wish I had waited in case I found something better. I did end up with a few colorful throw pillows and a blanket for the sofa-bed. Then I went to Costco and bought a new computer. I also bought a new filing cabinet since my old one was destroyed in the fire.

My next job would be going through all the kitchen, linen, and bathroom stuff Gideon and I had stored in the garage when we first decided to remodel the small bungalow. Thankfully, the fire hadn't touched the garage, so the things we had packed away were still there.

If Aunt Carrie had her daughter and granddaughter move into her home, I wasn't sure there would still be room for me. She only had three bedrooms and one bath in the small bungalow, which would mean that April and Joey would have to share a room if I was there too.

As these thoughts went through my mind, I looked around my office and decided that I could live in my office while my house was being restored. Why not? I had a shower, a stove to cook on, a microwave stored somewhere in the garage, and I could easily buy an apartment refrigerator.

My mind made up, I went over to Aunt Carrie's house and started packing my stuff. No need to wait. I was eager to start my life over on my own terms and in my own space.

Aunt Carrie wandered in as I was packing and eyed my movements somewhat cautiously. I looked up at her and wondered where she had come from since I hadn't seen her when I arrived.

"Well, well. Were you just going to leave without saying good-bye?"

I ran over to her and gave her a hug, "Of course not. I didn't see you when I came in. I thought you had gone out to one of your many social events."

Aunt Carrie was a social butterfly. Her midwestern hospitality and cheery disposition made her a welcome guest everywhere, and she was an awesome bridge player. Everyone wanted her as their partner, not to mention that she always brought something scrumptious to eat.

"I got inspired to go back to work today. After listening to your issues with April, it felt good to be helping someone, you know? I need to get off my pity pot, which is what Franny has been trying to tell me for months. It's time."

"But, where will you go?"

"Not far, I'm going to live in my office."

"Are you sure? It's not very big. How will you cook in that tiny kitchen?"

"You know I don't really cook. It will be fine. Don't worry about me. I want you to have the space to offer April and Joey a safe home."

"Is that why you're leaving? You think they need more space? Because if it is, I can assure you there will be plenty of space in my house."

I looked at her and sighed. "I'll miss living with you. I do love it here, but it's time for me to go. You've been so supportive. I don't know what I would have done without you. Besides, I'm right next door. If I smell something wonderful coming from your kitchen, I'll just invite myself over."

With that, she laughed and said, "You better. I'm going to miss you being around, but I guess if April and Joey come, I won't get lonely."

Oh dear, I had totally missed the fact that she might have been lonely. Maybe that's why she kept such a busy social schedule and never urged me to move out. I felt ashamed that I had been so self-preoccupied that I didn't even think of how Aunt Carrie might be feeling. I even excluded her when I isolated myself in grief after Gideon died.

I took her hands in mine and looked into her eyes and said, "You are like a real mother to me. I will always make time for you and am so happy you live next door to me. You have saved me these past six months. I want you to know that you are everything to me. I love you, but it's time for you and April to reconnect. This is such a great opportunity for that to happen. She's finally leaving Alex and you can be her rock now."

I had made a mental vow to myself to check in on Aunt Carrie frequently after I moved out. At sixty-eight years old, she had lost two husbands, then left her Midwest home and a lifetime of friendships to be with her daughter who, for whatever reason, had not paid much attention to her, nor allowed her to be much a part of Joey's life.

As I finished packing, I did hesitate, wondering if I truly was ready to start back to work. Was I really over my own trauma enough to be able to help anyone else with theirs?

Chapter 3

Moving into my little office space had felt exhilarating but a little lonely. I decided to call Franny and ask her to celebrate with me. We decided to go to the Alibi Room, a cozy little bar in Culver City. They had an outside bar with delicious small plates, mostly Mexican food, and the tables were set far apart so we'd have privacy.

Coming from Santa Monica, Franny picked me up on her way. We did small talk in the car, saving our celebration for the Alibi Room.

After ordering our drinks and a few small plates to share, Franny finally said, "Okay, MJ, what's the celebration for?"

I sat up as tall as I could at my five-feet-three, looked her in the eye and announced, "I'm going back to work."

After a moment of stunned silence, Franny raised her arm and pumped her fist as she let out a huge, "Yahoo!"

The shout coming out of Franny's mouth was so unlike her that I looked around a bit embarrassed and said, "You've been holding yourself back around this issue haven't you."

"Now look, MJ, I never wanted to push you, but I know you. You can't really sit around too long without a purpose, and we all know your purpose is to help people. Going too long without doing your therapy thing, or something else that helps people, was going to cause a lot of problems for you."

Our drinks arrived and I held up my cosmopolitan for a toast, "To going back to work." Franny picked up her very dry vodka martini with three olives and we clicked glasses. The chilled cosmo went down very easily. I closed my eyes and enjoyed the cool liquid as it slid down my throat.

We got to talking about how I should decorate my office, where I was going to get clients, and fees I needed to charge. But that was old stuff that I'd done before and the topic wore itself out pretty quickly.

After ordering another round of drinks, I said, "So, Franny, what's your next move? Planning another trip? What?"

Franny was a multimillionaire and didn't need to work, but she was always busy doing something. She loved to travel and owned several houses in various beautiful places, mostly near some body of water.

Before Gideon died, she had decided to start a relationship coaching business. This hadn't gone over well with me. I had spent time and money to become a licensed psychologist and she was just going to announce herself a relationship coach. I was upset and angry which led to us not talking for two years. The murder of Joe brought us back together and we've been working things out between us for the past six months.

Franny had admitted that she didn't know what she was doing as a relationship coach. She made a big mistake with one of her male clients. When this client threatened her, she bought a gun which she now carried on her person. I hated guns, as did she, and felt really uncomfortable around her when I knew she was carrying. Since she hadn't heard from this guy for over a year, I thought she should let it go. But her paranoia remained in tact. He had really spooked her.

"Nothing going on right now, MJ. I think I need a passion project to keep me motivated. Going to charity events and helping raise money for my pet projects just doesn't do it for me anymore. I liked the idea of being a relationship coach because it felt real to me. I could get my hands dirty, so to speak, you know?"

I did know. She had so much money she didn't know what to do with it all and often lost her connection to real life. I believed this was why she hung out with me. I live hand to mouth, never asked her for money like many of her other friends, and am committed to helping people with their emotional traumas. Franny wanted something like this in her life, but the coaching wasn't appropriate for her. She needed to find something that would allow her to engage with more of the underbelly of life. She had it too comfy.

When I started to order another round of drinks, Franny looked at me and frowned. "I think we've had enough, MJ."

"You may have had enough because you're driving, but I'm going to have a couple more. Come on Franny, don't be a downer. I'm finally going back to work. I'm celebrating moving into my office and starting to live again."

I was aware that the alcohol was making me more verbose than usual, but I also knew that I was drinking in order to not feel the creeping loneliness I would face at living alone again.

She smiled and agreed that it would be okay for me to have one more cosmo.

But it wasn't okay. I quickly drank two more cosmopolitans and had hardly eaten anything from the two small plates we ordered. When we got up to leave, I started to spin. I grasped the table and took some deep breaths, but the spinning did not go away.

It was bad. Franny hated when I drank too much and I didn't want her to see me this drunk, so I told her to wait while I used the restroom.

Once in the restroom, I turned on the tap and drank heavily from it, trying to stop the spinning. Three cosmos on an empty stomach. Would I ever learn? I hadn't been out much drinking in the past 6 months because I had been given some Xanax to help me through the extreme anxiety I was experiencing after the near death incident.

I had been tapering off the Xanax and since I hadn't taken any before we went out, I thought I'd be okay to have several drinks, but my system wasn't used to it after six months of abstinence. I clung to the bathroom wash basin trying to steady myself.

I had no idea how long I was in there drinking from the tap when someone finally banged on the door shouting to hurry up. I dried my mouth and stumbled to the door, still spinning. But what else could I do?

Franny met me at the door, took one look at me, and silently offered me her arm. I was grateful and also knew that she was miffed at having to do this again.

I didn't throw up on the way home, but the spinning never stopped and I felt awful, groaning and moaning for her to stop jerking the car.

"MJ, I am not jerking the car. You're drunk again. I thought you weren't going to do this anymore."

I heard the disappointment in her voice and wished I could have gone back in time and stopped at two drinks.

"Franny, I'm so sorry. I'll never do this again. I swear."

But I could hear echos of the same kind of promise my father had given over and over again as he slurred his words, much like I was doing.

"You've sworn this before and now look at you. You need help. Maybe you should go to AA. You liked that one meeting at the church, right?"

Oh dear, we were actually going to have that conversation about me being an alcoholic again. "What do you want me to do, Franny? Go to 12-step meetings? Never drink again? We love to go out and have a drink. Are you saying you never want to do this with me again? Because that's what it would be, if I get sober, I'll never be able to take another drink. Is that really what you want, Franny?"

As drunk as I was, even I could hear the defensiveness in my voice.

Chapter 4

Ugh. I woke with another hangover. I had been told not to drink while taking Xanax for my anxiety. As long as I was using the pills, I didn't have a need to drink alcohol. I sat on the side of the sofa, my head pounding, and remembered the disappointment in Franny's voice.

I had to seriously consider that I did have a drinking problem. It's come up for me before in the past couple of years, ever since Gideon died. After all, I was the one who demanded he have the liver transplant that led to his death.

Add to that, my father was a raging alcoholic. By raging I don't mean nasty or angry. He was sweet and kind of mushy when drinking and my mother hated it. This caused me to side with him again and again. But he just couldn't quit drinking, even after trying many times. He finally ended up killing himself one night, cutting through his arteries, leaving a massive amount of blood in his wake. He hadn't expected me to find him. I know he wouldn't have done it if he had known I'd be the first one to come upon him.

There is a part of me that still believes that maybe he didn't kill himself; that maybe someone murdered him. I still couldn't believe that he would do that on purpose, leaving me to live alone with my hateful mother.

I walked over to the kitchenette and drink gobs of water to satiate my dehydrated body. I was smart enough to know that alcohol and Xanax did not mix. So if I could control my drinking because I knew better than to mix the two, didn't that mean I wasn't an alcoholic?

I heard the denial and defensiveness in my own arguments with myself and knew that it would be a good thing to go to an AA meeting. Besides, I liked Big Al and always felt better when I was around him.

It was still early and I could make it to the 8 a.m. AA meeting at the church where Big Al presided. I met him when Joe, the man who was murdered, asked me to come and meet him. Big Al is referred to as 'The Priest' by AA members. But he told me he did not like the reference, so I think of him as Big Al; because he's big. But I just call him Al to his face.

Just before I was almost murdered by Detective Slatter, aka, Mike Rimichi, Big Al had given me the information I needed in order for Joe's murderer, Mike Rimichi, to be prosecuted. Big Al had put the incriminating evidence in an envelope and hidden it in an AA Big Book. That's why I now had a copy of it on my shelf.

He had tricked me into going to a second meeting, hoping to get me to start going to regular meetings. How he knew I had a drinking problem I never really knew. Maybe he could sniff it out. But being in denial, I never went back to a meeting after I killed Joe's murderer with a crowbar. Things felt settled after that so I didn't understand why I would need to go to a meeting.

After getting drunk the night before, I made the decision go to the morning AA meeting, if nothing more than to pacify Franny.

***

I hadn't been to the church for over six months, but nothing had changed. When I walked into the room, the large coffee pot was resting on the table in the back of the room, with various types of creamers and packets of Sweet and Low and real sugar. Donuts, crescents and cookies took up the rest of the table. People were milling around the back, grabbing coffee and sugary treats to eat as the meeting was about to begin.

As before, Big Al lumbered up from the back, nodding to people and shaking hands. He didn't see me since I was hiding in the last row, trying my best to avoid any kind of eye contact. I still felt embarrassed about being there and didn't want anyone who may know me to see me there. It didn't even occur to me that if they were there, then they were alcoholics too.

Big Al started the meeting promptly at 8 a.m. The 12 steps and 12 traditions were read, followed by a request for any announcements. Then Big Al introduced the speaker, who was an old timer with forty years sobriety. I thought to myself that I would kill myself if I had to go forty years without a drink. I had a hard time imagining going to parties, or just going out to eat without at least a glass of wine.

The speaker talked on and on about how he might take a drink tomorrow, but he wasn't taking one today. Well, good for him. My negative attitude was showing and I was resenting Franny for making me feel guilty. Who was she anyway, judging me? After all, I didn't judge her for spending money on frivolous things when that money could better be used to help people who didn't have as much as she did.

When the meeting came to an end and we stood and held hands as we said the Serenity Prayer, I looked up and saw Big Al looking at me. He gave me one of his big welcoming smiles, and I knew I wasn't going to be able to slip out unseen.

He was instrumental in helping me bring Mike Rimichi down so he could never sell the dangerous steroids to bodybuilders again. I was drawn to Big Al. He was like a big teddy bear, big but gentle. He had a checkered past. I didn't know the specifics, but I knew he killed a guy and that he spent 15 years in prison for something else he wouldn't talk about, at least not to me.

When we connected, he wrapped his big arms around me and pulled me close, saying in his big voice, "I knew you'd make it back."

If felt like the entire group was staring at us and I flushed that crimson flush of embarrassment that I've had my whole life and never been able to control.

"Hi, yourself. And don't count your chickens; this is just a one time visit."

"Oh really? Hey, let's go over there and sit down a sec. I want to know how you've been."

He grabbed a cup of coffee and about three donuts, indicating for me to do the same. I selected an almond crescent and watched him go over to the side wall where he found us a couple of chairs.

He was a very popular sponsor and leader of that AA group, so he had several people wanting his attention. I waited patiently while he made arrangements to call or meet with his followers, then went and sat across from him as he popped a donut, whole, into his big mouth and chewed for a minute, chasing it down with a large gulp of coffee.

"So, how've you been, MJ? I heard you were pivotal in taking down a drug lord."

I laughed at his exaggeration. "He wasn't a drug lord exactly." Rimichie was a slimy manipulator who had an illegal business making tons of money selling pharmaceutical grade steroids through a cache of unethical and amoral doctors who wrote out prescriptions without seeing the bodybuilders, causing all kinds of bodily harm, plus the death of a young man.

"Okay, okay, I stand corrected. So why are you here, MJ, if not for the AA meeting?"

My emotions took over. Sitting across from Big Al, I felt the tears coming and I could not stop them, "I don't know. I drank a lot last night and my best friend thinks I need help."

"And what do you think?"

I couldn't look him in the eyes, so I looked down at my hands and said, "I can't stand the thought of never, ever having another drink, you know? Alcohol has been my constant friend. Who will be there for me if I can't drink?"

"Hey, listen up. You don't need to never drink again. You don't need to declare yourself an alcoholic if you don't want to. Why don't you just come to these meetings a couple of times a week? Just come, have a cup of this god-awful coffee and your favorite pastry. Think of it as going out for breakfast. I'll be here to talk to you and I'll even give you my number if you need to talk. How does that sound?"

I looked up at him. I'm not stupid. I knew what he was doing, but I appreciated it and reluctantly nodded my head yes.

Chapter 5

The first thing I did after I left Big Al was to call Franny and tell her about me going to an AA meeting. I hated it when we were upset with each other and I knew she'd forget about her disappointment if she knew I went to a meeting. I wasn't sure if I was going to go back or not, but Big Al and I exchanged telephone numbers, so I assumed he'd probably call me. He did say that I didn't have to think of myself as an alcoholic, nor did I have to stop drinking.

At least, that's what I thought he said.

Franny was elated, as I knew she'd be, so we got to talking again about me starting back with my psychotherapy business. I decided that I'd go ahead and call my therapy colleagues to let them know I was resuming my practice and that I'd been getting help with the PTSD and all was well.

This wasn't exactly true, but I wasn't going to tell them I was still anxious at times and still had trouble sleeping. No one would refer clients to me if that was the case. I also decided to drop an ad into my professional magazine and call all my old friends again to let them know I was back in practice again and doing well.

After the incident with Mike Rimichi, it was all over the news and of course my old friends had called, mainly to get the gossip, I figured, but I did appreciate their concern. At first, their concern helped me reconnect with them, but then I isolated myself at Aunt Carrie's house because it was all too much for me.

Since I'd moved into my little office space, I felt like working again. It was also cool that I could look out my back windows and see the progress that was being made on the renovation of my little house. I could also make sure that they paid attention to my little fledgling lemon tree and kept heavy equipment away from it. It was the tree I planted for Gideon after he died and I was very attached to it and excited that it was actually producing lemons.

In the mean time, I set to work getting my new computer set up, along with setting up a new charting and filing system for my clients since my computer and all my files were destroyed in the fire.

Maybe having all of it go up in smoke was a good thing. It felt like I was starting over on a clean slate, so to speak. I was using money I got from the hazard insurance to live on, so I knew I'd have to start building my practice and making money soon or I'd be in a terrible financial bind again.

I felt my phone vibrate in my pocket and when I looked to see who was calling, my pulse definitely sped up.

It was Jesse.

I answered in a voice that I hoped sounded casual. I hadn't dated since dating Gideon years ago and it was all new to me.

"Hey, MJ. How's it going?"

"I'm good. I'm good. And you?"

Gees, it was like we were both being extra polite and it felt awkward. I'd visited him a lot when he was in rehab, but once he got out and we started seeing each other outside the rehab center, our relationship took a turn toward more intimacy, which produced a certain awkwardness in both of us.

"I was wondering what you're up to tonight."

Tonight? I hadn't told him that I had just moved back into my own place. And since he was still camping out at his friends place, we hadn't had any privacy yet. The thought of us alone in my space made me very nervous, but also excited.

"What do you have in mind?"

"Thought we could grab a bite to eat at Paco's. I'm so bored sitting at this desk here, I need a little excitement."

"Oh? And Paco is such an exciting place?"

Paco's had been around forever with a large clientele, so one usually had to wait in line. They had a woman making fresh cooked tortilla's as one walked into the restaurant. A huge fish tank with exotic fish swimming around in it was in the center of the room. Since it was November, they most likely had Thanksgiving decorations everywhere. It was an institution and the food was good. I loved the place.

"I was thinking more about the company I'd be with if you accept my invitation."

There was a suggestive hint in his remark, but I couldn't think of anything witty to say. I wasn't very good at flirting, unless I had a couple of drinks under my belt.

Paco's had great margaritas, so I accepted the invitation, totally forgetting that I had just been to an AA meeting.

***

Jesse beat me to the restaurant and had put his name on the list so it didn't take long to be called for our table. Once seated, Jesse quickly ordered a pitcher of margaritas and knowing I'd be fortified with a drink, I was able to relax a little.

Jesse started in on how boring his desk job was and that he might actually die of boredom. Before I could say anything, he reached over and took my hands in his and said, "God, it's good to see you."

I could feel the blush coming on and wished the waiter would hurry up with the drinks. Jesse was a very intense man. Before he was shot and I was seeing him as a client, I had a difficult time keeping my feelings for him at bay. I had a crush on him and had to work hard on my counter-transference. It was so intense that I had almost dropped him as a client.

In general, a therapist needs to wait at least six months before having a personal relationship of any kind with a client after therapy has ended. It had been six months since I stopped seeing him as a client, but I had gone to visit him in the hospital and then again in the rehab center. I felt like I owed it to him since he got shot trying to figure out who murdered my Joe.

"It's good to see you too, Jesse," I stammered.

He grinned his big toothy grin at me and letting go of my hands asked what I wanted to eat. I usually just got a bean burrito with a lot of sour cream, but when I told him my desire, he laughed and said that I needed to live it up a little and suggested the fajita's.

***

The margarita's definitely hit the spot and in no time we were chatting and flirting and making innuendos about whose place we'd go to. We joked about the sofa he was using at a friend's place and when I told him I had moved into my garage office space and had more of a loveseat sofa, we joked about which sofa would be more comfortable, all the time never admitting why. I didn't tell him that my sofa made into a bed.

This time, I was smart enough to know what my drinking limit was and stopped at two margaritas. Besides, they were a little weak, so I just got into my happy place buzz without getting loaded. Jesse seemed fine and we lingered a bit, ordering coffee after our meal which sobered us up. The joking about whose place we'd go to ended.

After leaving the restaurant, we stood on the sidewalk, both of us acting a bit awkward when Jesse finally asked where I had parked my car. It wasn't far away and when we got to it, he leaned in to me and gave me a kiss on the mouth which shocked me a little. It shouldn't have, since we had been joking about going to one of our homes after dinner, and it seemed as if we were headed toward a more intimate relationship.

I looked at him, and when he didn't make any other move toward me, I turned and unlocked my car door. It was confusing and I wasn't sure if he was leaving the next move to me, or if he didn't want to pursue it any further. So I opened the door and got in as he closed the door behind me.

Driving home, I felt confused and a little bit frustrated. Was I just a friend in his mind? Someone to do something with to pass the time, to help with his boredom until he fully recovered? But then why would he have kissed me on the mouth?

By the time I got home, I was feeling vulnerable and exposed. The flirting and suggestions had turned me on, something that I hadn't allowed myself for the year Gideon was fighting his liver cancer and the year after he died. Jesse was the first man that had held any interest for me since Gideon.

I found a spot to park in front of my house and as I got out and slammed my door, I saw a car come and pull up beside me. I felt the familiar panic start to rise inside of me. I felt trapped. I froze until I saw Jesse get out of the driver side and come around toward me.

I let out a huge sigh of relief and as he came closer, I felt the adrenaline leave my body. I grabbed hold of my car to keep me steady. He reached for me and all the tension that had been building up between us for months got released. I grabbed hold of him and felt the strength of his muscles under his jacket, and the heat between us.

***

We've all seen the sex scenes in the movies where the couple, for the first time, end up ripping each other's cloths off as they fervently kiss on their way either to the bedroom where he throws her on the bed, or they end up standing as he lifts her up and braces her against the wall while they have passionate sex.

Well — that didn't happen.

Instead we had an intense make out session in the middle of the street that got interrupted by a car honking at us as it tried to get around Jesse's parked car that was in the middle of the street.

"I just wanted to make sure you got home safely, MJ. I hope we can do this again real soon."

I watched as he hurried to move his car and was a little disappointed that he hadn't asked to come up to see my new place. But he did say he hoped we could do this again. It gave me something to look forward to.

Chapter 6

It felt like nothing could bring me down after Jesse and I made out after dinner the night before, so when Franny called me with her request, I was happy to oblige. Especially since I had decided to take on a client load and start my practice again.

She asked if I could see someone she had seen before when she was trying to be a relationship coach. His name was Luke Brown, was in his late thirties, and had called her to reconvene his sessions. He had disappeared after only coming for a couple of sessions with her.

As it turned out, he had stopped his sessions because he had felt guilty for not paying. Since Franny wasn't a licensed provider, she wasn't able to take his insurance. She had waived his fees since she didn't really need the money. He still wanted to pay and knowing he couldn't afford her fees, asked if he could pay part and owe the rest.

It seemed odd to me that he couldn't figure out how to call his insurance and find a therapist who took it, and I wondered how he had found Franny in the first place.

Franny had told him that she was no longer in business as a relationship coach, but she knew someone who could take insurance and was very trustworthy. Me.

She told me that he still lived in his rent controlled apartment in Santa Monica. It was actually a guest house behind the main house in a less trendy area. He told Franny he was still living with his two female roommates and still worked in a warehouse in downtown Los Angeles.

He had originally requested her services because he was having romantic feelings for one of his roommates at the time and wasn't sure how to proceed, so he needed a relationship coach.

As Franny explained a little about him, I understood why she had a soft spot for him. The way she told it, he was a large man, most likely around six foot eight, but with a gentle childlike quality; innocent, trusting, and vulnerable.

It felt good to start working again, even though I would only be getting a low fee from insurance. When Franny reassured me that he had insurance, I said, "Okay then, Franny, give him my number. I'll talk to him and see what I can do."

***

Not more than ten minutes later, Luke called me and we made an appointment for that very afternoon. It was going to be my first client in my new office overlooking my house. I had been excited about working again. It felt like my life was being renewed and I was going to embrace the good.

Over the years, people have often asked me if I wasn't scared working out of my home with possible "crazy" people, but I had never had an issue with clients until about six months ago when one of my clients transferred all of his feelings from a deceased wife on to me and started making trouble by involving Jesse, who was also a client of mine at the time.

However, if it weren't for this troubled client stalking me, I'd be dead now. So, no, I don't fear for my life from my clients, but I do need to remind myself to keep very good boundaries with them. Besides, I told myself, this client would have stalked me no matter if I saw him in my home office or an office somewhere else.

I'm usually pretty good at determining if a client would be dangerous when I first talk to them on the phone even before I see them. And most of my clients were women; so I don't, as a rule, fear any bodily harm from them.

Franny had told me that Luke was like a big gentle giant and that reassured me. So, at the time, I didn't have any fear of him coming to my home office.

Chapter 7

Once Luke was seated on the sofa across from me, I saw a large man with light brown skin, short kinky black hair, clean shaven face, and large brown eyes. He was dressed casually and neatly with workwear khaki pants and a fitted dark green olive sweater, along with brown Skechers boots. When he looked at me, he showed an open face with a dazzling smile and looked much younger than his thirty-eight years.

I smiled back and said, "It's nice to meet you, Luke. Outside of seeing Franny, have you ever been in therapy before?"

"No ma'am, I haven't."

No one usually calls me ma'am and I was impressed by his good manners and respect, even though it made me feel really old.

"I'm detecting a slight accent, Luke; where are you from?"

"Born and raised in New Orleans."

"Ah, I see, and what brought you out to California?"

Luke shifted in his seat and as his smile disappeared, a frown formed on his forehead and he didn't answer the question, but just stared at me.

At this point, I was just making casual conversation in order to bond with him and to make him feel comfortable, but clearly I had hit a nerve and made a note on my notepad to come back to it later. At the time I hadn't felt that this information was pertinent, but the way he stared at me felt uncomfortable.

"Luke, if there are things that make you feel uncomfortable in here, it's okay to let me know that you're not feeling like talking about it. Part of the therapeutic process is to help you feel safe with me, so that you can eventually talk about things that you've never been able to talk about, things that are difficult for you. Everything you tell me in here is confidential between you and me, and the goal is for you to feel safe enough to deal with some of those inner demons."

Of course, I then had to go on and explain what I couldn't keep confidential, like child and elder abuse, if he is a danger to himself or others, or information I may be obligated to disclose to his insurance company in order to get reimbursed, and finally, court subpoenas. I wasn't totally clear about what I was obligated to disclose in a court of law, because I had never been subpoenaed and didn't intend to ever be. So was rather vague about that one. I figured that if I ever had to go to court, I'd have an attorney there to tell me what to do.

His smile returned and he seemed to relax a bit, and so did I. I didn't press him to tell me why he came to California, but instead asked him about his family and how it was for him growing up since this was a significant part of my intake for clients.

His smile disappeared again and he looked straight at me and asked, "What is it you need to know, because my family is gone."

"Oh, I am so sorry to hear that. Can you tell me a little more about that?"

"They are all gone, and I don't like to talk about it."

There it was again, the frown and him evading a question that was quit pertinent and usual for a therapist to ask. However, I realized he had never really had therapy before and I would have to circle around to this information at a later time. I made another note on my legal pad to ask about his family at another time, and put a big question mark next to it.

I was curious, though, about his family. Were they gone, as in dead, or, was his family estranged from him? Since it was clear that he really didn't want to talk about it, I rather assumed that something happened between them, and so he wasn't in contact with them anymore.

There was a discomfort in the room and I had started to feel like maybe I shouldn't take him on as a client. But he looked me in the eyes and smiled his dazzling smile and I shook the discomfort off as I asked him why he was seeking therapy.

He told me what I already knew, that he had had romantic feelings toward one of his female roommates, Sahara, when he had first gone to see Franny. We were in comfortable territory talking about relationships because that was something that I was very good at dealing with; for others, not necessarily for myself.

"I see. Are the two of you in a relationship now?"

"No, Ma'am. She and Joy, my other roommate, have been smoking marijuana. When they became roommates, the rule was that there would be no smoking in the house, and no drug use, but I know they've been smoking because I can smell it when I get home in the morning."

Luke explained that he worked the night shift at a warehouse, getting home around 8 a.m. every morning.

"I believe my body is my temple. I don't put anything bad into it. I don't use any kind of drug, and I eat clean. I work out every day, and I don't want to be smelling that stuff when I come home. I can't be with a woman who does't take care of her body."

I was curious about his strong beliefs and asked him if they were because of a certain religious bent.

"No ma'am. I don't go to church."

Waiting for more details as to why he was so particular about his body, he remained quiet, so I asked him what it was that he needed help with.

He told me that he wanted them to stop smoking in the house. There was a certain naïveté that I was picking up as he spoke. It seemed like his thinking was more like a child than an adult and I could see how Franny got the impression of him being a bit childlike.

I then asked him if he had any kind of legal or written agreement about the no smoking in the house rule, to which he answered that they had a verbal agreement to that effect. The girls had been friends and had come to live with Luke at the same time after they had lost their apartment a year or so prior. He had an agreement with his landlord that he could rent out the other two bedrooms in the house, but the lease was in his name. He'd had the place for about fifteen years and had always had roommates and never had a problem with any of them until he rented to Sahara and Joy.

We discussed his living situation and I questioned him about how he asked them to comply with the house rules, but he continued to go on and on that he just wanted them to stop smoking in the house.

At the end of our time together, I was still unclear about taking him on as a client, but found myself taking care of the insurance information and his co-payment, and explaining things that I couldn't keep confidential. He signed my agreement and we made another appointment for the following week. We agreed that it would be his standing appointment time and that we'd meet weekly.

I asked for a name and number in case of emergency, telling him that it was usually a family member.

He did admit that he had a half-brother, Aaron Haas, but claimed he didn't have a telephone number for him and had little to do with him. Upon further questioning, he also admitted that Aaron lived up north with their father, Otto Haas, who owned orange orchards. Luke's mother had not taken Haas for Luke's surname, but kept her last name for her son, Luke.

So he did have family in California. He denied having any numbers or contact with his father and half-brother, but gave me the name and number of his friend John, who he worked with at the warehouse. He didn't seem to have John's last name, which seemed odd to me.

After Luck left, I felt like there was a lot he wasn't telling me. I realized I had a sick feeling in the pit of my stomach. I get these intuitive instincts a lot, but never know if they are real ominous feelings of things that will actually occur, or just old fears that surface whenever I get triggered a certain way, especially after the last incident with Detective Slatter, aka Mike Rimichi. I wasn't sure I could trust myself again in judging a person's character.

Even though I made another appointment with Luke, I wasn't sure it was a good idea. I was both drawn to him and repulsed at the same time, but felt helpless to make the decision to not take him on as a client.

Chapter 8

After I made my professional notes in Luke's chart, I couldn't shake the uneasiness I had after the session. I went over to Aunt Carrie's house to distract myself, and found her in the kitchen as usual, making dinner.

"Sit, sit."

She always made extra, so I sat and let her serve me a bowl of chili and piping hot corn bread with butter and honey on the side.

Comfort food.

"Oh man, Aunt Carrie, just what I needed."

"I'm so glad you came over, Honey. I have something to tell you, but first eat, eat."

"What's going on?" I asked, as I cut myself a large piece of corn bread and drizzled honey on it after slathering a good portion of butter.

"April and Joey are moving in soon," she said with a wide grin on her face.

My smile matched hers and I said, "I'm so happy for you. Do you feel better now?"

"I do, and I'm delighted I'll get to really know my granddaughter now. I've been out shopping all day today to buy her presents. Alex never allowed me to do that for her and I'm making up for it now. Besides, what else do I have to spend my money on?"

I laughed with delight and blew on my chili before I ate a spoonful of the spicy, thick stew. I closed my eyes and almost groaned with pleasure, it was so good and wondered again how Aunt Carrie could make the simplest meal taste like heaven.

"When are they moving in?"

"I'm not sure, but soon. She's really scared to move all of her stuff out of their apartment in case Alex comes around. From what I understand, he's under the impression that she's going to take him back."

"Aunt Carrie, did April get a restraining order against Alex?"

"Why, I don't know. I'm not even sure I know what that is."

After explaining it to her, I told her that she might want to help April get one, especially if she's afraid of him. I surmised that there must be a lot more to their relationship than she was telling Aunt Carrie. Women who are abused, and I should know, often hide it due to shame and fear.

We ate our meal in silence, both of us contemplating what we had just talked about. I couldn't help but think about Luke. Even though he didn't tell me what happened to his family, I felt a dread creeping into my consciousness. I didn't want to cause any unnecessary fear in Aunt Carrie, so I kept my mouth shut. After all, I had come over in the first place to try and get the session out of my head.

For dessert, Aunt Carrie offered me a piece of fresh warm apple pie just out of the oven, and I accepted. I mean, if you've ever tasted her fresh pies, you'd eat it too. I did, however, refuse the ice cream.

***

Feeling full and satiated, I made my way back home. It felt funny calling my office my home, but it was quickly becoming familiar to me and I imagined it's what living in a tiny house would feel like. I realized I needed to order a refrigerator and go through my kitchenware stored in my garage to find my microwave and other things needed in order to cook a little so I wouldn't keep begging from Aunt Carrie. Especially once April and Joey moved in.

Contemplating her fears about April caused me to put Luke's session out of my mind. I decided to call Jesse to get his take on how April should proceed.

He answered after the first ring with a simple, "Hey."

I was momentarily speechless, realizing that I hadn't thought it through; calling him, I mean. Would he think it was an excuse to call him after our make out session? Was it an excuse?

"Hey," I said, "I have to ask you some professional advise."

He hesitated before replying, "Shoot."

After I explained April's situation, I heard him emit a long deep sigh and then he spoke in what I took as his professional voice, "MJ, you need to tell her to get a restraining order as soon as possible. I'm serious. I would not trust that guy. I see this kind of thing all the time. These guys never stop. Almost three women a day are killed by their partners."

"Jesse. I. . ."

He cut me off, "Tell her to go down to the courthouse and get that restraining order. Then have her call a moving company to move her. You call me as soon as she has the time and date and I'll be there with my uniform on. He comes to give her any trouble, he'll have to deal with me!"

"You'd do that for her?"

"Of course, MJ. As a therapist, you know as well as I do that this is a critical time for her. She just threw him out; he's the most dangerous right now. Especially if he sees her moving."

I knew this and had suggested to Aunt Carrie to help April get a restraining order, but the way Jesse put it, I became alarmed. I thanked him and told him I'd make sure it happened and I'd call him with the time and date for the move.

After I called Aunt Carrie and got her reassurance that she would persuade April to get the restraining order the next day and would let me know when the movers came, I felt better. I left a message on Jesse's phone that it would be taken care of the next day. I also thanked him for offering to come and protect her.

That taken care of, I went on my computer to look for apartment size refrigerators. I measured the space and the doorway to make sure I could get one up the stairs and into the office, and ordered a red one.

I thought about going into the garage storage to find my microwave, but it was getting late and I was tired. I turned on my iPad and started watching reruns of one of my favorite sitcoms when I felt the buzz from my phone.

It was Jesse.

"Hi."

"Hey, MJ. I got your text message. I'm sorry I was so forceful with you earlier. I just didn't want anything to happen to your friend, April.

"Yeah, you did come on a little strong, but I appreciate the urgency of your message."

"I know that sometimes I come on really strong and it turns people off. It's just that I get upset when women don't take offensive action against these guys. It could save so many lives."

"Jesse, I do understand; you're talking to one of those women who had to learn to take offensive action."

There was complete silence on Jesse's end and I waited for him to respond.

His voice was soft when he finally said, "I didn't know. You seem so put together. I would have never thought you had been in one of those abusive relationships."

"Well, now you know."

I was feeling vulnerable and wasn't sure I even wanted to share that part of my life with him. I had a habit of denying it and keeping it hidden in the shadows. When he didn't respond, I felt even more uncomfortable and wished I had kept my mouth shut.

"MJ?"

"Yeah, I'm still here."

"Just the thought of some guy hurting you makes me want to beat the crap out of him."

"Jesse, it was a long time ago. I'm stronger now and know it will never happen again. No need to worry about me."

"I know you can take care of yourself, but I also feel protective of you."

"You do?"

"Yeah, I do. Can I tell you something?"

"Sure."

"I had actually been disappointed when I answered your call earlier and you asked me for advice. When I saw it was you calling, I had hoped you were calling to get together with me."

Wow. I did not expect that. Here I was feeling embarrassed about sharing my vulnerability with him, figuring he'd think less of me and he was actually sharing his own vulnerability. It made me like him even more.

"Jesse. I used my friends' dilemma as an excuse to call you."

He laughed at that and said, "Well, I guess we're even."

After we hung up, I felt soft and loving inside. Then I saw my notes about Luke lying on my desk and a feeling of dread came over me at having to see him again.

Chapter 9

The next morning, I woke early and decided that it would be the day I'd finally go through all of my stuff stored in the garage. After fortifying myself with several cups of coffee, I rummaged through my things to find utensils and cookware to bring up to my tiny kitchenette.

Looking through all of our things brought on a bit of sadness and nostalgia remembering how Gideon had refused to throw anything away. However, I was able to shake that feeling off as I found our microwave and other necessary items and lugged them up the stairs to my little flat.

It was kind of exciting to have all the items needed to start my new life. All I needed was for my refrigerator to be delivered and I'd be all set.

It was late at night before I finished and realized that I hadn't really eaten, so I splurged and ordered take-out from my favorite Thai restaurant.

Flopping on the sofa, I turned my iPad on to find something funny to watch when I heard my cell phone buzzing next to me. As a psychologist, I couldn't allow the ringing of a phone to interrupt a session with a client, so I kept it turned off. This kept me from being tied to my phone, but it also had me missing calls, sometimes important ones.

When I looked at who was calling, I saw it was Jesse and that he had been trying to reach me since early morning and I hadn't even checked my phone.

"Hey, MJ. I was beginning to think you were avoiding me."

"No, no. Not at all, but it's been a heck of a busy day.

"Tell me."

"You don't really want to know. It involved really exciting stuff like going through boxes and boxes of stored stuff."

"I get it."

Since we had opened up to each other with our true feelings, neither one of us really knew what to say; so there was an awkward pause.

"Look, I know it's late, MJ, but I've been thinking a lot about you since the other night outside your place and then again about our conversation last night. Any chance I could come over?"

"Now?"

I looked at the time. It was 10 p.m. I was a dirty mess and hungry, still waiting for my take-out to be delivered. I hadn't showered and had kept my nighttime sweats on all day long. I couldn't allow Jesse to see me the way I looked and I paused a moment to ask myself if I had the energy to shower and change so late at night. Besides, this was a late night call, and I wasn't sure if this was a booty call or not. I didn't want to take the chance that if I said yes and it was nothing but a booty call, then I'd feel really awful about myself.

The fact that I was actually taking time to look at the consequences of my actions was new to me. I was usually impulsive and didn't think before I acted. Or, I acted as a reaction to my emotions.

"Hello, are you still there?"

"Um, oh, sorry, I um, um. . ." I stammered.

"Hey, MJ, I don't want to put you on the spot. I get it. It's late. I had tried to call you earlier to get together, so let's leave it for another time, okay?"

I let out a sigh of relief. "That sounds like a plan, Jesse. I'm a dirty mess right now and have had a very long and physically trying day, but I'd love to see you another time."

However, he hadn't suggested another time and I was disappointed by that. I wondered if he felt rejected. Maybe I should have let him come, or I should have suggested another time.

There I went again, trying to take care of everyone's feelings, neglecting my own. It was late, damn it, and I was tired and hungry and not open to entertaining a man I was crazy about. I spent time reassuring myself that I deserved to say no and if he couldn't take a no, then, well, it was just too bad.

I thought I had wrestled enough with these old worthlessness feelings, but apparently not.

The food came just then, and I ate heartily as I watched "Curb Your Enthusiasm," so I could get a good laugh, as well as, watch a character that was more neurotic than I.

Chapter 10

The next week seemed to fly by and my refrigerator finally came. I can't explain how excited I was to have one. Now I didn't have to constantly go out to eat, or order in. Who was I kidding? I mostly ate at Aunt Carrie's house, who was so excited about April and Joey moving in that she could hardly contain herself.

She did insist April get a restraining order and it looked like things were finally settling down for her and Joey. Aunt Carrie told me she was helping them pack their stuff and sorting through what needed to be stored and what needed to come to her house. She figured that they'd be ready to move in the next week.

Jesse hadn't called me again and I was impatient waiting for April to get a moving date, so I'd have an excuse to call him and to see him again. It bothered me a lot that he never called back, but it bothered me even more that I was acting like a lovestruck school girl, sitting by the phone waiting for her crush to call her.

***

Lukes next appointment seemed to come very fast. I had managed to put it out of my mind until the morning of. I got up and attempted to do the stretches I had committed myself to doing as well as take my morning walk to the beach and back. But, I just couldn't force myself to take the walk. Instead I drank copious amounts of coffee in order to keep myself from falling into despair.

Since I had decided to start taking on clients again, the only one I had managed to get was Luke, and now I wasn't feeling so good about seeing him. It had only been a week and I knew referrals wouldn't come to me right off the bat, but I was still feeling down and sorry for myself.

When it was finally time for Luke's session, I had worked myself into a caffeinated frenzy and wasn't sure I was going to be able to focus. But I did feel that I was quite professional when I found myself sitting across from him.

He smiled his dazzling smile and I found myself relaxing into my chair as I asked him how his week went.

His face took on a look of puzzlement as he talked about his roommates.

"Dr. Lange, I just want them to stop smoking marijuana in my house. How do I get them to stop?"

"Luke, have you asked them to stop?"

"Sure. I tell them all the time to stop."

"So, you've told them to stop, but you haven't had a conversation with them about your verbal agreement that there would be no smoking in the house?"

"What do you mean?'

"Well, we can't just tell people to stop doing what they are doing. We need to have a conversation around the topic."

He looked at me with the same puzzled look, so I suggested that we do some role play.

"What do you mean, role play?"

"Okay, Luke, it's like I'll be you and you be one of the girls. We'll pretend we are having a conversation with me pretending I'm you, and you pretending you are one of your roommates. Does that make sense?"

I felt like I was talking more to maybe an eight year old.

"Oh, I get it. Okay. I'll be Sahara."

He looked at me in anticipation so I suggested that I start, as Luke.

"Hey, Sahara, do you have a minute to talk with me?"

Luke just sat and stared at me.

"Luke, I'm pretending to be you, I just asked Sahara if she had a minute to talk. You need to answer in the way Sahara would answer, because you're being her."

"Oh, okay. Ask me the question again."

"Hey, Sahara, do you have a minute to talk to me?"

"Yes, I do."

"Well, I am aware that you and Joy have been smoking marijuana in the house and wonder if you remember our agreement that there would be no smoking in the house?"

Again, Luke sat in silence and I had to prompt him that he needed to answer as Sahara. I wasn't sure the role playing was going to work. I didn't get the impression that Luke had a low IQ, but it was more that he wasn't getting the social cues.

"Maybe, Luke, you should just tell them that the agreement was that there would be no smoking in the house and that they are breaking the agreement."

"Dr. Lange, that's what I am telling them, to not smoke in the house. It's really bothering me. A lot. I keep my home in impeccable order and the smoking disturbs that."

"Have you talked to your landlord about this? Could he help you deal with the rules of the house? I'm not a lawyer, but I seem to remember that there are laws about no smoking in rentals. I know people can't smoke in apartment buildings, except in designated areas. Surely, a landlord can dictate if there is smoking on his property or not."

I had no real facts to back this up, but I was trying to empower Luke to find solutions to his problem.

We spent the entire session around the issue of how to get his roommates to stop smoking, so by the end of the session, I hadn't yet asked him what happened to his family. We made another appointment for the next week.

I hadn't gotten such a strong negative reaction to Luke during the second session, but it was frustrating working with him. I didn't know if he was really that obtuse, or if he was pretending to be. I also got a strong sense that he might have some OCD disorder since he mentioned how he kept his home in impeccable order.

***

The next few sessions with Luke didn't seem to go any easier and I decided that maybe he should get tested for autism, or some kind of learning disability. I was not trained to work with these issues and needed to know what I was dealing with. I just knew that it was very frustrating to work with him when he didn't seem to understand the most basic ways of conversing.

He still hadn't allowed me to question him about what happened to his family and how he ended up living in Los Angeles. I felt more and more like I wasn't getting anywhere with him and was thinking that I'd have to refer him out if he kept evading my most basic questions.

At the next session, I was determined to take control of the session and get a proper history from him, but he started in the minute he sat down.

"Dr. Lange?"

"You can call me MJ, Luke. Most of my clients do."

"Yes, Ma'am. You know, I think Sahara and Joy are having parties in my house while I'm at work."

"Oh? What makes you think that?"

"Well, the house is a mess when I get home in the morning."

"Oh? And what do you do about the mess?"

"I clean it up."

"You clean it up? You don't ask them to clean it up?"

"No, Ma'am."

"Why is that?"

"They just laugh at me and make fun of me."

"How do they make fun of you?"

"They tease me about being a 'neat freak' and being a little old lady."

At that point I saw a tear fall down his cheek and realized that his roommates were making life miserable for Luke.

"Oh, Luke, people can be so mean and hurtful," I felt like I was talking to a child and even though he was a large man, he seemed like a little kid and my heart went out to him.

I could see the hurt inside of him and could relate to how painful it was for him when his roommates were cruel to him. At that moment I decided that I wouldn't be able to refer him out. I felt his pain and wanted so very much to help him lessen the pain.

So we continued to meet every week and I continued to try and help him communicate better with his roommates. I tried to help him find solutions to either get cooperation from them, or to see if there was a way for him to legally end his contract with them.

We also discussed his preoccupation with messes around him and I was more and more convinced that he had some kind of OCD. He was compelled to clean and needed things to be kept in a specific order in his home in order to feel comfortable. I understood this, but

I could see how hard it would be for someone to live with a person who couldn't tolerate any kind of a mess, be it large or small.

However, the more he shared with me about the cruelty and disregard for his needs by his roommates, the more I felt a growing dislike for them, and the more I wanted to protect Luke.

Chapter 11

I had been seeing Luke for several months, and by now had finally gotten several more clients. All my attention wasn't consumed by him anymore. Then one morning I woke up to a buzzing sound coming from my phone. I found it embedded somewhere on the sofa bed and saw that it was a call from an unknown number. I could also see that it was 9 a.m. and I had overslept.

I jumped up, phone in hand. The buzzing stopped only to start again a few seconds later at which time I was able to answer. "Hello, this is MJ Lange, may I help you?"

"This is Detective Nordell from the Santa Monica police department. Do you know a Luke Brown?"

Just hearing the word Detective put me into some kind of an altered state and I flashed back on Detective Slatter/Mike Rimichi, the man I killed. I felt myself spinning, eyesight dimming, pulse racing, and my mouth go so dry I couldn't speak. I was clearly having an anxiety reaction just by hearing the word detective coming from the deep and official sounding voice. My trauma therapist was helping me identify my triggers so I would be able to handle them better, but I didn't need any help identifying a trigger around a police detective.

"Hello, Ms. Lange, are you there?"

"I. . . I'm here, yes, I'm here. Hold on a minute and let me put my earbuds in so I can hear you better."

My hearing loss was bad, but I found that the earbuds worked very well when I was on the phone. After I searched and found them and placed them in my ears I said, "Who did you say you were again?"

"This is Detective Nordell," he said, enunciating every word in order to make sure I understood him. "I'm calling about a Luke Brown. He said I should call you."

Luke, oh my god, Luke. Something happened to Luke. Was he all right? Had he been arrested? I couldn't bring myself to even ask; my mind was all over the place.

"Ms. Lange, are you all right?"

"Yes, I'm fine. What happened? Is Luke okay? Has he been arrested? What's going on?"

"I'm not able to tell you over the phone, but Luke is in a state of shock. He's being transported to the Santa Monica Hospital as we speak. You can find him there. We may need to contact you later, but for now, you're the only one he was able to provide a telephone number for."

"Of course, of course. I'll head over there now. Thank you for letting me know."

Not bothering to change out of my sweats, I rushed to use the bathroom and looked in the mirror to make sure I wasn't too disheveled. I grabbed my purse and hurried to my car.

Before I turned on the ignition, I sat for a moment and tried to remember to utilize the tools I knew could help calm me down. Deep breathing. Breathe in for a count of four, hold for a count of four, release for a count of eight. I did this until I could feel myself return to a more normal state and then started my car and drove purposefully to the Santa Monica Hospital.

I had no idea what to expect once I got there. I couldn't imagine what could have happened that would put Luke into a state of shock. It was almost 10 a.m. He must have arrived home from work around 8 a.m., if I was remembering right. Could he have interrupted a party by his roommates? Was there an overdose? Why was he in shock?

I continued to breathe deeply as I tried to find a parking space for the hospital. Plus, I wasn't sure where they had taken him. I decided to try the emergency room first.

***

After running around the hospital area, I finally found the emergency room, where I was told Luke was being seen by a physician. He had just arrived, they said, so they couldn't yet tell me anything about what was going on.

"Can I go see him? I got a call from the police and they told me to come here to be with him."

"Are you a relative?"

"No, I'm his psychologist, Dr. Lange." I don't like using doctor as my title, but I felt it was going to be the only way I'd get in to see Luke. Most people responded to the word doctor thinking that the "doctor" needed to be taken seriously in case of a life or death situation. We were in the emergency room, after all.

She looked at me with suspicion since I had on my sweats and my hair was a mess, and said, "Just a moment, let me check for you."

I waited for her to return and decided that if she didn't let me in, I'd call Detective Nordell back and have him make her let me see him. I couldn't stand the suspense. My mind was going wild with various scenarios, each one worse than the last.

When she finally returned, I looked at her anxiously and she told me that Luke was okay and I could go in and sit with him until the doctor released him.

Released him? So nothing was really wrong? What was going on here?

She led me into his little cubicle. It reminded me of Jesse's ICU room at UCLA when he was recovering from his three bullet wounds that Mike Rimichi had pumped into him. My trauma therapist reminded me that various things could trigger a PTSD response, and that I should try and anticipate a trigger ahead of time.

I thought the hospital would trigger something, but I was just relieved to see that Luke was okay. He was lying on a gurney type of bed, the head of the bed rolled up, so he was semi sitting, his face a grayish hue. A large blood pressure cuff was wrapped around his large muscular bicep. There was no one in attendance, so I guessed he must have been okay.

When he saw me come toward him, he attempted that bright, dazzling smile, but it didn't really work and he closed his eyes.

"Luke, what happened? Are you okay? Did they think you were having a heart attack or a stroke or something?"

He just looked at me and I noticed big tears running down his face and he looked away.

Feeling helpless, I took his hand and squeezed it saying, "It's going to be all right. It's going to be all right. We'll figure it out together."

I don't know why I said that. I had no idea what was wrong with him. I shouldn't have promised him anything until I understood what had happened. He looked like a child lying on that gurney, all alone, tears streaming down his face, unable to tell me what happened.

Chapter 12

We must have sat there together for about half an hour when Luke finally fell asleep from the shot they had given him. And it was his usual sleeping time so he must have been exhausted. I still didn't know what had happened and he had refused to talk about it. He didn't want me to call anyone, telling me there was no one to call.

I was getting hungry and wandered out to the waiting room where I found some machines and bought myself a cup of lukewarm coffee and a bag of vinegar and sea salt chips. I was surprised they let me take them in to where Luke was being observed.

Nurses kept coming in to take Luke's vital signs, and at one point a doctor came in to check on him, but wouldn't answer any of my questions, causing me much frustration.

Finally, I looked up and saw a tall, muscular man enter the cubicle we were in. He was dressed casually in brown chino pants, brown dress shoes shined to the hilt, and a dark green blazer over a long sleeved white shirt, giving him a casual, relaxed, but authoritarian stance.

He was followed by a short, stocky man wearing a police uniform, and the doctor that had come in earlier. He smiled briefly at me and asked if I were Ms. Lange.

"Yes, I am. And you are. . . ?"

"I'm Detective Nordell. We spoke on the phone."

Finally I was going to get some answers. I glanced at Luke who hadn't moved a muscle and looked very peaceful in his sleep. I nodded at him to continue.

"How are you related to Luke?"

"I'm his psychologist. I've been seeing him for a couple of months now. I'm not sure why he asked for me. Did he have an anxiety attack and that's why he asked for me? I'm in the dark here. He was unable to tell me what happened because they had given him a sedative. I have no idea what's going on and none of the staff here is answering any of my questions."

Detective Nordell spoke softly, "Can we speak outside, please?"

I followed him out to the waiting room where it was noisy and crowded, so we went outside and sat on an isolated bench. With the cool temperature, no one was sitting outside and we had complete privacy.

"We were unable to find any family of his since he was in shock and unable to tell us, and were hoping you'd be able to give us that information."

"Detective Nordell, I've only been seeing him a couple of months. He told me his mother's side of the family are all gone, but he did say that he does have a half-brother who lives up north somewhere, managing an orange grove."

"Ok, good. Do you happen to have the name and number of his brother?"

"I believe he said his name was Aaron or Adam Haas, it started with an A. I remembered the last name spelled H-A-A-S because I had needed him to spell it for me. He denied having a telephone number for him. You could find him with your resources, right?"

"Okay, thank you, you've been very helpful."

He stood and it looked like he was about to leave, so I said, "Wait just a minute. What happened? Why is Luke in shock, if that's what it is? You can't just leave without telling me what happened."

If they couldn't get hold of his brother, I wasn't sure what my responsibility was for Luke. I vaguely remembered that he had put down a friend's telephone number for emergencies, but I didn't have it with me. I'd have to go look it up in my intake notes.

"Fair enough, although I can't go into all of the details with you. I'm sure, that as Luke's therapist, he'll be able to give you more information. But I can tell you that Luke came home from work around 8 a.m., his usual time, and found both of his roommates murdered, lying in a pool of blood in the living room."

I raised my hand to my mouth and starred at Detective Nordell. My mind was trying to make sense of what he was saying.

"I don't understand. Who would do such a thing?"

I then had a horrible thought, "You don't think Luke did this, do you?"

Detective Nordell looked at me and didn't say anything for a few moments, most likely trying to decide exactly what all he could tell me before he said, "Well, we need to do more investigating, but based on our very limited initial investigation, it doesn't much look like Luke could have done it. He was in such a state of shock; we couldn't get much out of him. We'll need to interview him more extensively when he's doing better. And we'll have to wait to find out the time of death of the victims and see if it's even possible for Luke to have done this, since we already know he was at his job until 7 a.m. If that's the case, it would have been pretty difficult for him to have managed all of this in the short amount of time he had once he left work, but we aren't ruling anything out at this point."

I thanked the Detective and went back to sit by Luke's side as he slept in what I thought may be his last moments of peace. I had grown quite fond of Luke in the months we had been working together and it pained me to think that Luke may be under suspicion for these horrendous murders, and even though I was only about four years older than he was, it felt more like he was a child to me. I couldn't even imagine this polite, gentle man doing anything violent. I needed to know what happened — in his words — so I waited for him to wake.

***

When he finally woke, his first response when seeing me sit beside him was to offer his dazzling smile. Then he saw the look of concern on my face and remembered what had happened.

"Luke, how are you feeling?"

He turned his head from me and said, "I don't know. Dr. Lange, why is this happening to me? Why would this happen again? It's a nightmare."

"Can you tell me what happened?"

He took a deep breath and started to explain what happened after he got off of work and arrived at his home, but just as he got to the part where he found the bodies, the doctor came in and did an exam.

"You seem to be out of the woods, Luke. I'm going to release you, but I need to know you'll be staying with someone for a day or two. Do you have someone you can stay with?" At this point he looked at me with his eyebrows raised in a question mark.

I stammered because I knew I couldn't have him stay with me, so I asked, "Luke, do you have someone you can stay with? A friend perhaps, or someone from work?"

"I can stay with John, from work. He has a house close to mine. He's nice. Sometimes he gives me a ride to and from work if we work the same shift. That way I don't have to use the bus."

"Is that the friend you put down for your emergency contact?

"Yes, Ma'am."

"Do you have his number?"

In the aftermath of the murders, Luke no longer was in possession of his cell phone, so I offered him mine to call his buddy and they set up a time John could come and pick him up. Luke wasn't scheduled to work over the weekend, but I had him call off for the next Monday and Tuesday. He worked with heavy moving equipment and I felt it prudent that he not rush back to work before issues about the murders were handled. This was all new to me and I had no idea how to handle any of it. I kind of wished I could just go home and forget about it.

Oh my god, he was involved in a double murder. Talk about triggers for me. I vaguely wondered if I should try to find someone else for him to work with since it was so triggering for me. But he looked so small lying so still on that gurney with tears in his eyes, I just couldn't desert him.

John couldn't come for a couple of hours and Luke told me that he'd be okay waiting for him. He kept telling me he was sorry for keeping me all day, and he didn't want to talk about it. He told me that he would talk about it later.

I couldn't even imagine how shocking it was for him to find his roommates lying murdered in a pool of blood in his living room, so I didn't press him.

I was, however, ashamed to admit that I actually hadn't felt so bad about the victims. I had grown to really dislike them after hearing so much about how rude and mean they had been to Luke. Still, that old doubt and discomfort I had about Luke in the beginning reappeared inside my gut when he evaded talking to me about what happened. It was like he shut a big, heavy door between us and that barrier was so strong, it couldn't be penetrated. It was just like when he evaded talking to me about his New Orleans family and how he got to Los Angeles from New Orleans.

Chapter 13

When John came, he was able to reassure me that Luke would be fine at his place and could stay with him as long as he needed. I knew I could leave then but I didn't want to go home and be by myself. I needed a good friend to talk to, so I decided to go to Franny's place. I didn't want to talk to Aunt Carrie and risk bringing her down from her joy of having her daughter and grand-daughter move in.

Franny is a good listener and the minute she saw me, she grabbed my arm and pulled me inside, sat me down in her casual living room, went to her wet bar and poured me a vodka straight up, not even bothering to add ice, and said, "Ok, MJ, what the hell happened?"

She was like that—very perceptive. She would have been a great relationship coach had she just gotten a little training about boundaries with her clients; but that boat had passed.

Like I said, she was a great listener and kept quiet as I related the story of Luke's murdered roommates. I didn't even think that I might be betraying a patient's confidence as I shared all the details from the moment I woke in the morning to the moment I arrived at her doorstep. She's always been my confidant and I completely trusted her to keep to herself whatever I told her. It's always been that way between us from the first time we met as roommates our first year in college.

"I can't even imagine what it must have been like for him to find his roommates bleeding on the floor in his house, can you?"

My whole body shuddered and I took another gulp of my vodka, closing my eyes and feeling the warm liquid burn down my throat.

"I can't, MJ, but I'm wondering if maybe this has triggered something more for you."

"What do you mean?"

I knew I was being defensive, but I couldn't help it. I didn't have to ask what she meant, because I knew what she meant. I had been the one who found my father lying in a pool of blood after they said he slashed his arteries, attempting and succeeding in killing himself. He had been an alcoholic, married to my tiny Irish mother, who was a shrew, forever disappointed in him. And disappointed in me, saying I was just like him.

Franny was one of a handful of people who even knew this about my father. I mostly never talked about it, even when drunk. She was the only person I allowed to even bring it up. She knew I still couldn't believe he killed himself, leaving me alone to fend for myself with my mother.

I knew she was probably right, but my denial system was strong and I told her to shut up and stop being a pseudo-therapist.

"I'm fine, Franny. This is totally different from what happened with my dad. This is a murder and my client found them. He's such an innocent kind of a guy. I think he might have some kind of a learning disability or maybe he's on the spectrum. He acts more like a child than an adult. But you already know that about him don't you?"

Franny knew when to quit about my dad and we discussed what it must have been like for Luke to have found his roommates. We wondered if he'd be allowed back in his house and if so, would he even be able to live in a house where a double murder took place?

We both wondered aloud if either one of us could do that and commiserated in our mutual sympathy toward Luke.

***

The next morning, I called Luke on his friend John's phone to see how he was doing and to see if he wanted to come in for another session after what happened the day before. He declined and said he just wanted to sleep. I reassured him that I was available if he decided he did want to come in sooner than his set appointment.

I couldn't help worrying about him. Finding your roommates bleeding to death on your living room floor is quite a traumatic event. But I couldn't force him to come, and wasn't sure I was even capable of working with this kind of violent trauma.

I spent the day organizing my mini kitchen and kept my phone in my hip pocket so I wouldn't miss the call in case Luke changed his mind about coming in for a session. And, I didn't want to miss a call in case it was Jesse.

Ah, Jesse. There is was again. After Franny and I had our second shot of vodka, we changed the conversation to what was going on between Jesse and me.

After listening to my worries about Jesse not calling again or asking me out for a later time, she said, "Look, MJ, you were right to say no. It sounds to me like it could have been a booty call. You did the right thing."

"Deep down, I know I did, but I'm aching for touch, and Jesse is the only man I've been attracted to since Gideon died. Would it be so bad to have participated in a booty call?"

"It would absolutely be okay for other people, but not for you. I know you, MJ, you're all about connection. You'd feel used and bad after a one night stand. It wouldn't work for you."

"I guess you're probably right, but do you think I should call him and apologize for not saying yes to him coming over that night? Explain to him why I had to say no?"

"Absolutely not, MJ."

"Okay, okay, Franny, don't worry, I won't."

I realized I was on edge with so much going on. I thought that maybe I should go to an AA meeting and wondered how that thought came up, especially since I had just downed two large shots of vodka.

Chapter 14

And so. . . I had driven home with two large shots of vodka in me. I should have been thankful that I wasn't picked up for any kind of moving violation because I'm sure my blood alcohol level was higher than legal. I did not go to an AA meeting, but instead went over to visit Aunt Carrie who was busy making her famous chocolate chip cookies. I was just sober enough to make a mental note not to dump my troubles on her.

She greeted me with a smile on her face saying, "April and Joey are coming over tomorrow to double check the space here so they know how much room they actually have to move into and to figure out what they have to put in storage. She wants to see the space again before setting the date for moving. She keeps worrying about the cost of the move, but I told her not to worry about the money because I'd pay, but she won't hear of it."

She looked so happy bustling around her kitchen and with my vodka buzz, I was happy for her and almost forgot about the tragic double murders.

"Aunt Carrie, it's a good thing she's trying to pay her own way. It shows she's a good person, reliable and dependable. She's been under the thumb of an abusive partner. Let her feel good about her independence and about taking responsibility."

"Ack, you're always right, MJ. How'd you get so smart about these things?"

I loved it when Aunt Carrie "acked" at me. It reminded me of my German father, who said it often, usually in reference to making light of a worry of mine. Aunt Carrie had a German heritage also, and some of her actions and words left me feeling safe and secure, just like I did as a young child around my father.

"These kinds of things are my business, Aunt Carrie. I can figure all kinds of things out for other people, but when it comes to my life, I suck."

We both laughed at that and she invited me to eat dinner with her, or as she called it, *supper* — the Midwest term for the evening meal.

I was happy for her excitement at having April and Joey come live with her. She deserved happiness and I hoped that April and Joey would become part of my life, too. I didn't know if I was a bit jealous of April and wished Aunt Carrie had been my mother, but I knew enough on how to handle my emotions around those kinds of feelings.

Usually, I just stuffed them down and that's probably why I drank whenever I felt uncomfortable.

After I left, I started feeling a little guilty about not going to an AA meeting, so I called Big Al and chatted with him a bit. He reminded me about the early morning meeting at the Church, so I had no excuse not to go.

I still wasn't convinced I was an alcoholic, and wasn't committed to going to meetings, but I also found myself being a bit at loose ends since moving into my office. There was nothing, or rather no person to ground me anymore. I was left to my own devices and it felt uncomfortable. I'd be sure and talk about this in my next therapy session with my trauma therapist. Lately we'd been meeting only every other week. She felt I was making good progress and didn't think I needed weekly sessions.

Here's the thing about me: I'm very good at showing a very healthy and positive front, but underneath, I hurt. I often feel lonely and lack confidence. I could fool any therapist I ever went to. It wasn't on purpose and every so often I did get help with my anxiety and depression, but as a general rule, I hated to feel vulnerable and usually kept up a good front.

As I contemplated all of this, I found myself pouring a shot of vodka and gulping it down, unconscious as to what I was doing. This was then followed by another shot, and then a third as I opened my sofa bed and drunkenly tried to make it up with the sheets that reminded me of Gideon.

I stumbled into bed without brushing my teeth or washing my face and was soon fast asleep, not seeing how automatic it was for me to just take the shots when I was feeling restless or out of sorts.

***

As I hurried into Big Al's meeting promptly at 8 a.m., I wondered why I had promised him I'd come. It was a beautiful day and the sun streaming into my window earlier had awakened me and I didn't feel so bleak anymore. I had time to shower and dress appropriately for the meeting. There was no need for breakfast because his meetings always had my favorite almond crescents. The coffee was bitter, but not bad after a bite of the pastry. Anyway, he had told me to come for breakfast, hadn't he?

I sat in the back again, trying to make myself invisible. I had a lot of shame around stating myself an alcoholic. I did not want to be like my alcoholic father, but it is a disease of denial, no denying that.

I laughed inwardly at my attempt at humor and smiled as I sipped my bitter coffee and ate my delicious crescent.

After all the preliminary prayers and rules, the man who shared was funny and interesting, telling hilarious stories of his drinking and using. At the end of his share, he became very serious and told us how he came to AA.

He had been drinking a lot one night and on his way home, as he drove over a hill, in his drunken state, he got confused and rammed into a car head on. The car carried a family. Both mother and father were killed, along with a little five year old child sitting in the back with her older brother and sister, who miraculously came out of the accident unscathed, except for the loss of their parents and little sister, of course.

I got up and left the meeting. This wasn't me. I'd never drink and drive. I was responsible. Anyone who drank and drove was an idiot and deserved to be put behind bars. Except, I had to admit that just the day before I had driven after two vodka shots in rapid succession.

My father never drank and drove, but he was definitely an alcoholic. In fact, I realized that I had never seen him drive, ever. My mother always drove. I don't think I ever saw him drive in my entire life, or at least from my earliest memory.

Having these kinds of thoughts are the only times that I wished my mother was still alive so I could ask her things I didn't know, like why he never drove. Could it be that he had gotten a DUI, or that he had his license taken from him permanently? Or, worse, did he have an accident where someone died? Was that why he kept himself numb? He couldn't tolerate the guilt of being the cause of a death?

I left the meeting feeling worse than when I started.

Chapter 15

When Luke came to see me for our next scheduled appointment, he didn't look so good. Gone was the dazzling smile, and he wore a worried expression on his face. He told me that they still had the police tape over the door, and he was still living with John from work.

"Have they told you anything like who may have done this, or when you'd be able to get back into your house?"

"No. They haven't told me anything. They don't know who did it. I can't stay with John forever. I need to get back into my own house. I need my clothes to go to work."

We talked about his support system, which wasn't much.

Then I asked him about his half-brother and his father.

"I don't have much to do with either one of them now."

"Have you ever?"

"I never knew my father growing up. When my mama got pregnant with me, he left us. I think he sometimes sent her some money. But that just gave her money to use more drugs."

At this he snorted in disgust and looked away.

"Have you ever seen your father, and do you know or have you had any contact with your half-brother? You know his name, so maybe you've been in touch?"

"Okay, my half-brother contacted me in New Orleans after my mama died. He had come to New Orleans to meet me. He had just learned about me from my father and wanted to meet me."

"So, he would have been just a teenager. Was he there alone, or with your father?"

"Aaron's four years older than me. Otto, my father, had him with a woman he was married to. They were separated when my father came to New Orleans and met my mama. Since he was still married to Aaron's mother, he couldn't bring my mama and me back to California with him."

"So your father got back together with your half-brother's mother back here in California?"

"Yes."

"So, he sent money every once in a while, but never attempted to meet you, or get to know you?"

"No. I guess he was ashamed of me, being of mixed race. He says that's not true, but I don't believe him."

"So, your half-brother, Aaron, came to meet you in New Orleans?" I asked to encourage him to continue.

"Yeah, Aaron came and found out that my family was all dead. He brought me out here to California."

So his family was all dead.

"You lived with your brother when you first came out here?"

"Aaron and my father."

"Your father was okay with that?"

"Aaron was angry at Otto for hiding me from him. He hated our father for not owning up to fathering a child with a black woman. He called our father a hypocrite and racist. He was angry because they hid me from him all his childhood when he could have had a brother."

"Wow, that must have been intense."

We both remained silent for a bit. I was absorbing all of this information. There was a lot to assimilate.

"How long did you live with your father and brother?"

"They felt sorry for me because I had lost my entire family. At first it was nice and I felt cared about."

"Even by Aaron's mom?"

"Yes, even her."

"Then what happened?"

"Aaron and Otto kept arguing about everything. It got really uncomfortable for me. I felt like I was the cause of their yelling at each other. After about a year, I left and came down here to Los Angeles and stayed. This is my home now."

"Did you ever feel like going back to live in New Orleans?"

He looked at me with soulful brown eyes and said, "I have nothing to go back there for but bad, bad memories."

"You mean, because you lost your family there?"

He just looked down at his hands and remained quiet.

When I tried to engage him again about what happened to his family, he remained silent, so I asked, "Do you still see your father and brother?"

"Half-brother," he clarified, "No, I never see Otto. Aaron comes down here sometimes and we go out to eat or to a sports bar to watch a game. Every once in a while, he gets us tickets to watch a hockey game in the winter. I don't care much for him. He keeps trying to get me to go to college, or to get a better job. But I like my life here.

I wasn't sure where to go at this point so I ventured, "Luke, do you think you could ask Aaron for some support at this point? Since you can't get back into your house and may not be able to stay with John for too much longer, maybe Aaron could help."

"No, I don't want to ask him for help."

"Why not? Seems like he cares about you from what you've told me. He seems to want to keep in touch and to connect."

Luke looked away and started fidgeting with one of the pillows on the loveseat.

I watched him for a while and then asked, "What are you thinking, Luke?"

"Nothing. Is my time up?"

It was and I knew there was something that Luke was hiding from me, or maybe he was hiding it from himself. He refused to talk about his family in New Orleans. I knew I shouldn't push him too hard if there was some serious trauma he had undergone, so we ended the session with an appointment for the next week.

As it turned out, luckily, I also remembered to get John's address so I knew where he was living for the time being. I was concerned about him and offered my support and availability during the week if he felt he needed extra time. He maintained that he didn't have his father's and brother's telephone numbers, but I wasn't sure I believed him.

The session left me drained. There was something about what Luke had told me that bothered me, but I couldn't put my finger on it. I really wanted a drink, but it was still early and I knew it wouldn't be a good idea if I started drinking during the day. I had done that after Gideon died, and it made my life worse, not better.

It had bothered me that Luke kept evading talking about his family in New Orleans. At least he told me they were dead and I wondered how they had died. It was like there were two Luke's, one with a delightful smile and engaging childlike quality of innocence, and another that was evasive and dark, holding secrets and detached.

I was feeling agitated, but didn't feel like writing up my notes for the session so I left my office and headed over to see Aunt Carrie.

Chapter 16

Aunt Carrie was digging in her garden when I got there, so I knelt down beside her and started pulling dried flowers and weeds.

Looking at me, she remained silent and kept her steady weeding, but after a time she finally stopped, looked over at me and said, "Are you just going to pull weeds, or are you going to tell me what's bothering you?"

Since I never offered to help her in the garden before, I guess it was obvious there was something on my mind.

"It's just a client of mine that has me going, that's all. I can't talk to you about it, but he has me kind of spooked and I need to focus on something else, so here I am pulling weeds in your garden."

She gave out a hearty laugh and reaching out her hand she said, "Here, give me a hand. Let's go inside and have some of those chocolate chip cookies with a nice cold glass of milk."

After helping her up, I followed her into the kitchen and sat at the table as she bustled around pouring us each a squatty glass of milk, and then set a plateful of the cookies in the middle between us.

We dunked the crispy cookies, laden with extra chocolate and walnuts, into our milk and ate in silence.

"Okay, my dear, what's really on your mind? You've been a therapist for decades, so don't tell me it's just a difficult client. I know you better than that."

How did she do that? It's like she reads my mind. That's probably why I love her so much. I've never had a person "get me" like she does, except for maybe Franny. But Franny's my age and a bit self-absorbed most of the time. Aunt Carrie always has some kind of comfort food available for me, and knows just what to say and what to ask that allows me to open up.

"Do you think I'm an alcoholic?"

"What makes you ask that?"

"Well, I really started drinking a lot after Gideon died, Franny thinks I'm one, and my father was definitely one. Just now, I wanted a drink after my difficult session. It's still day time and I'm wanting to drink."

She sighed and said, "MJ, I'm not here to judge you, but if you think you've got a drinking problem, then maybe you need to look into it."

I got up from the table and as I hugged her good-bye, I said, "Thanks."

"What for?"

"Just for being you."

She patted my hands and shooed me away.

***

After the cookies, I felt better and was able to write my process notes about Luke. There was still something that bothered me about the session, or rather what he was not saying, but I'd have to see where the next session took us.

I needed more clients, so set about making to-do lists of what had to be done in order to fill my practice.

It was dark when I finished and decided that I needed to get some real food in my stomach and debated whether I should go out or order in.

As I was debating this question, I thought of the dinner with Jesse and wondered if I had totally blown it with him since he wasn't calling me, but it didn't feel right for me to call him. I'd have to wait for April to pick a date she was going to move out of her place before I had a reason to call. I decided to order in and eat my pizza alone while watching something on my iPad.

I didn't feel like having a drink at all, so maybe I was making too big of a deal about me being an alcoholic. Maybe I had low blood sugar is all and the cookies got it back up. I'd have to watch when and how I ate.

***

The next morning, I woke early and decided that even though I wasn't sure if I was an alcoholic or not, I'd go to the 8 a.m. meeting.

I arrived early and when I entered the meeting, Big Al was already there. He grinned at me and managed to guide me to the front of the room after I got my bitter coffee and pastry. I glared at him, but he only threw his big head back and let out his famous rich laugh that filled the room. Heads turned to see what was so funny.

Again, I sat in the meeting with various conflicting feelings raging inside me, but sitting in the front made it hard to leave. Big Al knew what he was doing. He knew I wouldn't leave from the front row because it would call attention to me and that would be the last thing I'd want.

I hardly listened to the shares and became increasingly impatient as the meeting seemed to drag on and on.

When at last we all stood to say the Serenity Prayer, I scurried out the door before Big Al or anyone else could stop me. I left the meeting feeling worse than when I came, which was becoming a common theme.

Except I had no idea how bad the day was going to get.

My phone buzzed and I saw the name Luke Brown, so I pulled over and answered.

"Luke."

He didn't answer, but I did hear some heavy breathing, so I said, "Luke? Is that you? Are you okay?"

Still no answer.

"Luke, you need to answer me."

Nothing. I wondered if maybe he had dialed me by mistake and didn't even know I had answered, but I had a feeling that something wasn't right.

"Luke, you're scaring me. Please answer. I can't tell if you're in trouble, or if you dialed me by mistake."

There was a pause, but then I heard a weak and rather raspy voice say, "I can't take it anymore. It's all too much. I just wanted to thank you for caring about me."

Then nothing, even after I attempted to arouse him again and again by yelling his name.

I knew I needed to call 911 and ask for a wellness check, or to send an ambulance, but I didn't want to hang up on him either. I had no idea how to put him on hold with my cell phone and call 911 at the same time, so I made the decision to hang up on him and called 911.

After looking it up on my cell phone and giving the emergency operator John's address, I punched it into my Mapquest and headed over there also.

Chapter 17

I saw the ambulance as I approached John's house and knew I had done the right thing. After parking, I ran over to one of the policemen who was standing outside and asked how Luke was. But before he could answer, the paramedics came out the door with Luke on the gurney.

I ran over and walked beside the gurney as they rushed him to the ambulance. He was awake, but drowsy, and his speech was slurred.

"Where are you taking him?" I asked, then hurried to my car and followed them to Santa Monica Hospital, thinking that it was the second time that month that I was rushing to the hospital to see how Luke was doing.

What had I gotten myself into?

Knowing a bit more about the parking and the lay of the hospital, it didn't take me long to find where Luke was. Once again, in the emergency room, where I learned that he had taken all of his Xanax. There hadn't been that many pills for him to take, he hadn't used any alcohol, and being a big guy he was going to be okay, physically.

However, it was a suicide attempt, so they were putting him on a 72 hour hold, called a 5150, in which a person can be placed on a three-day hold against his wishes if he is a danger to himself or others.

This was serious and I knew that a psychiatrist would be coming to evaluate him. I didn't know how long it would take for one to get there. I decided to stay with him until one showed up so I could ask questions after the evaluation. I wanted another professional's opinion about what was going on with Luke. Once again, I wasn't so sure I was the person to be handling Luke's issues.

The staff was monitoring him closely for any signs of suppressed breathing, and told me that they didn't have to give him anything to reverse the effects of the Xanax. Apparently the amount he had taken wasn't a lethal dose and mostly made him sleepy, but Luke didn't know that.

Luke slept for a couple of hours and I found myself, again, going to find some coffee or chocolate to keep myself awake. I wished I had brought my kindle because going through emails on my phone didn't appeal to me.

I was very worried about Luke and wondered if I should refer him to a trauma therapist. Finding his roommates slaughtered like that had to have triggered a huge reaction in him. I wondered if I shouldn't have done more toward keeping him safe, but wasn't sure what that could have been.

I felt like I was working in the dark. I didn't have all of the pieces and it was driving me crazy. Usually my clients tell me their trauma history. Luke didn't give me much to work with. He avoided talking about anything that happened before he came out to California. Something had to have happened in New Orleans and I started to wonder how his family had died.

***

When Luke woke after a couple of hours, he looked at me in a mournful way and I stood up and took his hand, searching his face in hopes that he'd be able to talk to me about what he was feeling. I kept quiet and waited for him to speak.

Finally, he said, "I guess I'm still alive."

"Yes, you are. Talk to me."

After a huge sigh, he looked away and I saw tears running down his face. Even though he was a big man, he looked small and vulnerable and I wanted to hold him like a small child.

"Why is this happening to me? I don't understand. Why would people I live with get murdered like this again?" He then looked at me and said, "Doctor Lange, what's happening?"

I had no idea what to say. I didn't understand why his roommates were murdered either, but mostly, I didn't understand why Luke would try to hurt himself. Again, I thought there was something he wasn't telling me.

I looked at the clock. It had been four hours since Luke arrived in the emergency room. The staff kept checking in on him and taking his vitals, but still no psychiatrist.

Not knowing what to say or do for Luke, I told him I was going to go check on something and went to find a staff person who could tell me if a psychiatrist was coming or not. One of the nurses told me that there was a psychiatrist on call and she had been contacted, but sometimes it took a while before they were able to get there.

To be honest, I had not wanted to go back and talk to Luke. I felt helpless in the face of his trauma. But I also felt it was important that he not be alone and that he had someone to talk to. And I thought it was imperative that his father and half-brother be contacted regardless of what he wanted.

I stepped back into his little room and took his hand again and smiled at him, "What's going to happen is that a Psychiatrist is going to be coming to evaluate you. I believe they will put you on a 72 hour hold in order to stabilize you and make sure you aren't going to hurt yourself again."

He looked at me with alarm, "I can't be here for that long. I need to be at work. I can't get fired. What am I going to tell them?"

"Luke, you did a serious thing. You took all of your Xanax. Thank goodness you didn't have enough pills to do any real harm, but a suicide attempt is serious and we are all taking it very seriously."

I didn't want to mention contacting his family. I thought that during the three days he would have on his 5150 hold, someone would address that issue with him, so I was off the hook. I knew he'd most likely fight it and I didn't want to be the one bringing it up. He might take it as a betrayal from me and if I was going to continue to see him, I didn't want that to be an issue.

This was beginning to feel like an all-consuming client and I wasn't sure I wanted to continue working with him since he seemed so unstable. I generally stayed away from complicated clients, and mostly dealt with relationship issues or personal conflicts.

There was a lull in the conversation and just when I was about to break the silence, a dark haired rather pudgy woman who looked to be in her mid fifties, entered. She was dressed in a gray wool dress with sensible black shoes, but had a confident air about her as she strode purposefully toward us, stuck out her hand and introduced herself as Dr. Melissa Holden.

She looked at me with a question in her eyes, so I explained to her who I was and why I was there. I wasn't sure if I'd be allowed to stay or if I needed to give them some privacy.

"Luke, I'm here to do an evaluation on the state of your mental health. Do you understand?"

He looked at me and I nodded encouragement to him.

"Doctor Lange told me a psychiatrist would be coming to see me. Are you a psychiatrist?"

"Yes, I am. We all want to make sure that you get the help you need. I need you to be honest with me as I do the evaluation. I'm going to be asking you some questions and if you don't understand something, just ask and I'll clarify for you. Do you understand?"

He nodded his head yes.

Dr. Holden then looked at me and suggested that I could take a break and go get myself a cup of coffee or tea.

I nodded and as I was turning to leave, two very tall muscular men entered the cubicle. They looked almost identical, except the older man was about six inches shorter than the younger. They both wore washed out blue jeans, long sleeved heavy weight fleece button down shirts, and cowboy boots. All that was missing were the cowboy hats.

The older man was clearly in charge and with a booming voice said, “What the hell is going on here?”

Chapter 18

Both Dr. Holden and I looked at Luke. I thought I saw an initial look of fear in his eyes, but he either recovered quickly, or I was mistaken.

"Otto. Aaron. Why are you here?"

Realizing who they were, I offered my hand to the older man and introduced myself. Then I introduced Dr. Holden and repeated the same introductions with Aaron.

"So you would be Luke's father and brother."

"Yup, we are, and I demand to know what's happening here!"

Dr. Holden rose to his demand with equal self confidence, explaining why she was there. Otto responded emphatically, "Luke does not need a head doctor and we are taking him home — now!"

Dr. Holden responded calmly, "Luke is on a 5150 hold, which does not allow him to leave for seventy-two hours

I'm afraid. I'm going to do my evaluation now so maybe the two of you can go with Dr. Lange to the cafeteria and get a cup of coffee. I'm sure Dr. Lange can give you more information so you can make a wise decision."

She really put me on the spot; I did not want to be talking to Otto. He seemed like a bully and I don't do well with bullies. But Dr. Holden insisted that we all leave together.

I could see that Otto wasn't used to being bossed around and I could see his fists clench as a prelude to something more violent when Aaron spoke up, "Otto, let's let the doctor do what she has to do, then we'll have more information and figure out what needs to happen next."

He spoke in a calm, easy manner, but I could see that there was fire underneath all that calm, and didn't want to see what might happen if he were crossed. I also noted that he called his father by his first name and not dad, or father, or any other name of endearment.

The last thing I wanted to do was get coffee with these two cowboys. Then again, I thought I might be able to gather more information from them about their relationship with Luke. I also wanted to figure out what Luke was hiding from me about these folks, because I was sure he wasn't telling me the whole truth, or at the very least was leaving some important things out.

We headed out to the elevators and once inside I punched the ground floor knowing it would take us outside where there was more room to contain the angry energy emanating from Otto.

"Shall we sit at those tables over there and talk, or would you like something to drink or eat?"

Otto snarled at me and it took everything in my power not to cower under his glare. I looked at Aaron for help. He did not disappoint.

"No thank you. We're fine. Can you tell us how long it's going to take Dr. Holden to do the evaluation so we can take Luke home?"

I realized that they were determined to take him home no matter what, and I knew that Luke needed professional help. It didn't take much to assume he wouldn't get that help if he went with these two, so I tried a different tactic and attempted to keep my voice modulated in a concerned tone.

"I know the police were trying to find a number for next of kin but were having difficulty finding you, how did you find out about Luke?"

"A detective called us earlier today."

Otto chimed in, "Damn city cops. That thing happened days ago, why weren't we informed? Why didn't Luke call us? We're family, gol dern it."

I didn't know what to say. That he would call a double homicide a "thing" was interesting to say the least. I couldn't tell them that Luke didn't want them to know, or that he was hesitant about having anything to do with them. Or that he claimed he didn't have telephone numbers for them.

It was a mystery to me. Both Otto and Aaron seemed genuinely concerned about Luke. They seemed to want him home with them in order to take care of him like family. Support like that could solve a lot of Luke's problems.

If they did succeed in taking him up north, then he would no longer be my client. If he stayed here and I continued to see him, I'd definitely need some clarification as to why Luke was so put off by them. I had hoped that they would succeed in persuading him to go home with them so I'd be off the hook. The situation was getting more and more complicated and I did not think I was the one to sort it all out.

"Well, as you might imagine, Luke was in shock after finding his roommates murdered in the way they were. It takes a while to put it all in perspective, to even know what steps he should be taking."

This all seemed self-evident to me: they should already know how traumatized Luke would be. Before they could answer, I hurried on, "Can you tell me what you know about Luke and any prior trauma he might have had? Anything that could be helpful in his treatment."

Otto just scoffed and turned away, ignoring me, but Aaron said, "You must know about what happened to his mother in New Orleans more than 15 years ago, right?"

I assumed he was talking about her death, so I nodded to encourage him to continue.

"I tried to befriend him and bring him back here to live with us and he seemed to adjust just fine for the first year or so, and then he just left and moved to Los Angeles."

"Did he tell you why he moved down here?"

Ignoring my question he said, "I tried to keep in touch, to include him in things like Holidays, my wedding, the birth of my son — things like that. I also drove down a couple times a year to see him, but it was like a wall went up around him. I couldn't reach him."

"Did anything specific happen up there that could have triggered him leaving, or triggered him losing trust? Anything at all, no matter how small."

He just sat and looked at his hands clutched in front of him, not speaking.

On the other hand, I could see Otto seething and wondered why he was so angry. It couldn't just be that he was thwarted in taking Luke with them, could it? After all, from what Luke told me, Otto didn't have much to do with him the past fifteen years, so I wondered why he was even here.

We sat in silence, each in our own thoughts until Otto finally looked up at me and said, "Luke's probably told you that I left his mother soon after he was born and never had anything to do with him until his mother died."

I reminded silent, hoping that he would continue.

"Well, young lady, I have to tell you that if I had to do it all over again, I would have fought for him and brought him out here to live with me once I found out about his mother's drug abuse."

This was not new information about his mother's drug abuse. But I suspected he might be feeling some guilt, if he had any feelings at all. But he wasn't about to share that with me.

"Why didn't you?"

He took a deep breath and said, "Because I was young and stupid and I already had a son at home that I had neglected. I thought I was doing the right thing at the time."

This unusual show of honesty was said in anger which I assumed was there as a defense against his vulnerability.

I noticed that Aaron was fidgeting in his chair and looked a bit awkward. I would have loved to be a fly on the wall in that family over the years. There was definitely something going on between Otto and Aaron; I just didn't know what. Too bad they lived so far away, because if I was going to continue to work with Luke, I'd really want to do some family sessions with him that included Otto and Aaron, and maybe even Otto's wife, of whom I had heard nothing about so far.

"I assume there is a missus Haas?" I wanted to know what Otto's wife thought of all of this.

Having established that there was, I wondered aloud what she thought, when Aaron stepped in and said, "We can leave her out of this. She's suffered enough."

Obviously I couldn't hide the surprise I felt with this statement and it must have been written all over my face because Otto chimed in and clarified, "My wife, Isabelle, has advanced MS and spends most of her days in bed, or sitting in a wheelchair outside. She has lost her ability to walk, and has a great deal of difficulty talking. We have a live-in caretaker for her and we try to reduce all stress around her."

It was the first sign of softness that I saw in Otto. I suspected that he did have feelings for his wife and felt bad for her condition, but I also suspected he didn't have a clue as to how to go about dealing with any emotions he might have around her MS.

"Yeah, now you do this for her when she can't stand up for herself, or push back, or challenge you," Aaron sounded bitter and I wondered if this could be the issue that no one was talking about, or at least play a part in the drama.

"Aaron thinks that my actions caused Isabelle's condition. I wasn't a very good husband throughout the years, nor was I a very good father to Aaron. He blames me for everything that's gone wrong in his life, including his mother's condition."

I could tell that Aaron wanted to say more, but he was restraining himself. Otto went on, "But I was a good provider and now he, and Luke, if he'll accept it, will have high production orange orchards that they will be able to pass down for generations. That is my legacy and I'm proud of it. At least I did that."

Then he turned to Aaron, and said, "Someday you'll appreciate what I've been able to do for the family. You're just too pig headed right now. Guess you take after your old man."

"I'm nothing like you, old man, and I'll never be anything like you."

Whew, there was so much tension between those two that I wanted to get up and walk away. If this was going on when Luke lived with them, I could see why he left.

Trying to lighten the mood a bit, I asked Aaron, "Do you work on the orange farm with your dad, or do you do something else?"

Surprisingly they both chuckled a bit and I asked what was so funny when they said they'd never heard anyone call their orange grove a farm before.

I'm not a farmer or orange grover, or whatever it's called, but at least I succeeded in lightening the mood and they both explained to me their situation. They hired most of the work out, but both of them managed it together, supervising the maintenance and all that is involved — trimming, irrigation, mulching, and so on.

Aaron and his family lived a few yards away from the main house, so father and son lived very close to each other. Maybe it's true that familiarity breeds contempt. I was surprised that with all the animosity between them they lived so close.

I glanced at my watch and realized that Dr. Holden must be pretty near finished. I put my hands on the table, pushed myself up to standing, and invited them to come back up to wait in the waiting room until Dr. Holden was finished. Then we could see what her recommendation would be.

Chapter 19

When we arrived back at the nurses' station, the nurse at the desk went to see if Dr. Holden was still with Luke.

We didn't have to wait long when Dr. Holden came out and invited all of us to a smaller room where we had some privacy.

She took off her glasses and let them hang from an aqua-marine colored eyeglass strap, rubbing the bridge of her nose where her glasses had perched.

I was eager to know the fate of Luke, but I was more interested to know if I was going to still have him as my client, so I broke the ice asking for her verdict.

"Luke has suffered extreme trauma as a young man, or should I say teenager. This new trauma, that seems very similar to the first one, has triggered the old trauma. Adding the new to the old is a double trauma for him."

Speaking directly to Otto and Aaron she said, "I understand when he came out here to California and stayed with you after the first murders, he didn't get any therapy for the trauma or the grief of losing his family."

It was more of a statement than a question and Otto and Aaron didn't feel the need to reply.

What? Wait? First murders? What the hell? Was I hearing right?

She went on to explain that he was suffering from untreated Post Traumatic Stress Disorder from the first murders and that these new murders caused a re-traumatization that was putting him through a period of heightened sensitivity and renewed vulnerability to traumatic memories. Finding his roommates brutally murdered caused him to relive the initial trauma as if it were happening all over again in the present and he couldn't handle it. He was overwhelmed with stress and anxiety to the point where his only option was suicide.

She went on to explain that it was vitally important that he get the much-needed psychological treatment for the original, as well as the present-day trauma.

"Therefore, I'm admitting him on a 5150 hold in order to stabilize him, after which I am recommending outpatient trauma recovery therapy at the Santa Monica Service Clinic." She directed her next statement to me. "Dr. Lange, he seems to have made a strong connection of trust with you, so I am also recommending that he still continue to see you weekly as adjunct support.

"Any questions?"

Since I was still in shock learning about first murders, I found myself speechless. Dr. Holden's no-nonsense approach and emphatic decisiveness left little to be questioned, so Otto and Aaron also remained quiet.

As Dr. Holden turned to leave, I found my voice and took off after her, calling her name.

When she turned and looked at me, I blurted, "What first murders?"

"Luke didn't tell you?"

"No, he did not, although I did suspect he was hiding something. But, murders? Plural? Was his mother murdered?"

She took my arm and motioned me to sit down on a chair in the waiting room. I saw Otto and Aaron standing awkwardly off to the side as I looked into Dr. Holden's eyes and saw compassion and sympathy.

"Luke came upon his mother, her boyfriend, and his aunt all slaughtered in his living room after a high school football game. This happened when he was about seventeen years old, a senior in high school. He never told you?"

"No, he didn't."

My voice had dropped and all kinds of emotions battled inside of me. I flashed to the night Detective Slatter, aka Mike Rimichi tried to choke me to death and I ended up killing him and leaving him to burn.

I could feel myself spinning and didn't realize what was happening to me until I smelt a strong odor. Someone had cracked a capsule of ammonia under my nose after I had fainted. I came to and found myself lying on the dirty floor in the waiting room.

I looked around and saw Otto, Aaron, Dr. Holden, and a female nurse, who was holding the ammonia capsule under my nose, all staring down at me with mutual looks of concern.

My face flushed in shame at my inability to stay strong, so I shoved the capsule away and sat up telling everyone that I was okay, that I must have had low blood sugar since I hadn't eaten. I promised I would go get some food right away. I wanted them to stop fussing. It was embarrassing.

Dr. Holden looked at me curiously, handed me her card, and told me she'd be in touch to keep me abreast of Luke's progress and when it would be a good time to start seeing him again. She thought that would be close to when he got released from the 5150 hold in three days. She'd have him call me for an appointment and he'd also be in treatment at the Santa Monica Service Clinic for trauma. She'd make sure he signed all the authorization forms so we could keep in communication with all of his providers.

"Now, go get yourself some food. You scared everyone here."

I had to say that I really appreciated Dr. Holden for her take-charge attitude and felt like I could work with Luke as long as she would also be handling his case.

I stopped in to say good-bye to Luke, reassuring him that we'd be seeing each other soon. I passed Otto and Aaron on my way out and overheard them arguing in quiet but heated voices. I had no idea what they were arguing about. Dr. Holden had told them in no uncertain terms that Luke would be hospitalized for his 5150 and that was that.

I was exhausted and still needed to eat. I knew that my fainting wasn't just low blood sugar but that the entire murders I just heard about had re-traumatized me as well.

What I probably should have done at that point was call my trauma therapist and make an appointment as soon as possible. But, being me, I figured there wasn't anything she was going to do for me that I couldn't do for myself. I got in my car and drove to California Pizza, ordered a BBQ chicken pizza to go, along with a piece of red velvet cake.

My plan was to put the entire day out of my mind, gorge myself with pizza and cake, and then fall asleep as I read a book about the new happiness therapy on my Kindle.

It was a good plan and I didn't even obsess about the fact that Jesse still hadn't called me. I went to sleep and slept the night away without any alcohol.

If I could go without a drink after a day like I just had, then I wasn't an alcoholic. Or, at least that's what I told myself.

Chapter 20

Since Luke was in the hospital and I didn't have my other clients for another week, I didn't have much to do the next day until Aunt Carrie called and told me that April had set her moving date.

I was ecstatic because then I had a reason to call Jesse, and most likely a reason to see him since I was going to be helping with the move. The problem was that it was for the next day and I worried that he wouldn't be able to get away without prior notice. But at least I'd have a reason to call and talk to him.

I felt nervous because I knew in my heart that something was up with him or he would have called me by now. I put the call off while I busied myself cleaning my little bathroom. Finally, I could put it off no longer. I had to call him because it was my job to let him know when and where to go when April moved.

Taking a deep breath, I dialed. When he answered, I almost hung up; I was so nervous.

"Hey, Jesse," I said, "remember when you told me to call you when April was moving so you could be there in case her boyfriend showed up and caused trouble?"

"Yeah, I do."

"Well, it's tomorrow."

Silence on the other end. I waited and when I didn't hear anything I said, "Hello?"

"Dang, MJ, I can't do it tomorrow."

"Okay, I was wondering if you maybe needed more of a heads up, so no worries. I'm sure we'll be fine."

"Um, listen, MJ."

I didn't like the tone of his voice. It sounded like he was about to impart information that I did not want to hear, so I put him off and said, "Jesse, don't worry about it. It's going to be fine. After all, she has a restraining order and Aunt Carrie, myself, and the movers will all be there, so I doubt Alex will try anything. But, hey, thanks for offering in the first place. See ya."

With that flippant remark, I hung up before he had a chance to say anything. I gently beat my head with two balled fists, saying to myself, "MJ, you are so stupid. He obviously has no interest in you anymore. You are such a fool. Stupid, stupid, stupid."

But my heart was aching. I felt bereft and vulnerable and very much alone. All my hopes that there was something there between Jesse and me went up in smoke.

But there was still a part of me that couldn't deny the energy that I had felt between us. I mean, I'm pretty sure I didn't imagine that, did I?

Well, here I was in my tiny garage apartment, all alone, with nothing to look forward to. I was approaching my 42nd birthday, no kids, no husband, no boyfriend. I barely had a career anymore. Wow, I was really getting into a pity party. I needed to get busy and do something quick before I sank deep into one of my depressive states. I decided I'd go over and hang with Aunt Carrie.

Good thing I did, because when I got there, she was struggling with turning over the mattress in her guest room all by herself.

"What are you doing Aunt Carrie? You can't do that by yourself. Here, let me help you."

She looked sheepishly at me and agreed that she had been over confident that she could single-handedly turn a queen size mattress.

After we finished and I helped her make the bed with fresh linen, she told me she was headed over to April's place to help her do last minute packing. When I heard this, I offered my help which she gladly accepted.

***

Once at April's we saw that the house was full of boxes, all labeled neatly and organized into two very distinct groups. The larger group was going to storage, along with furniture, and the smaller was going to Aunt Carrie's house.

I shook April's hand as she smiled a shy smile and thanked me for helping. Little three-year-old Joey was running circles around the boxes, excited as could be and chanting, "We goin' to gwamma's house. We goin' to gwamma's house."

She was a cute little thing, light blond curly hair swept up into a little bun at the top of her head, pink top, pink tights, and pink shoes.

I knelt down and caught her as she went past and said, "Hey, little one, I'll bet I know what you're favorite color is."

She giggled and looking me right in the eye said, "Pink, my favwit cowoe is pink."

I laughed with her and let her go to continue her running around in circles around the boxes as I asked, "Okay, what can I do?"

"Honestly, if you could just keep Joey occupied, that would be a tremendous help. The minute I pack something, I turn around and she's unpacked it. I don't know how she does it. Maybe you could take her for a walk?"

"Sure. You got it."

I called out to Joey and the two of us left the house, hand in hand, to go for a walk in search of pink monsters.

It was a delight to skip along beside this little bundle of energy, but a part of me felt that old ache that I never got a chance to have a child with Gideon. But before I got into morose thinking, I reminded myself that I had come to help in order to get out of a depression, not to get deeper into one.

Joey and I had a long walk, or rather a stroll, as we stopped every few feet to either pet a cat, smell a flower, or pick up a piece of colorful trash — treasure for the little three-year-old.

By the time we got back to the house, they had finished what needed to be done and were sitting out on the porch waiting for us to get back.

"That was fast," I said.

"Yeah, Mom and I almost had it all done already, but thanks to you watching Joey, we were able to finish it up in record time."

April and Joey were going to follow us back to Aunt Carrie's. They were spending their first night there since all their beds were dismantled, ready to be hauled to storage the next day.

April thanked me again and I told her I'd see her tomorrow. "Oh, by the way, Jessie, that cop who offered to help, won't be able to be there. He needed more notice, but I'm pretty sure we'll be okay, right? Alex hasn't given you any trouble has he?"

"No, but we're due in court in a couple of weeks to get child custody figured out so he can't afford to do anything wrong."

Aunt Carrie and April gave each other a withering look at the mention of child custody. Alex would be granted visitation rights and maybe even 50% custody. The California family courts were prone to give 50/50. I felt for April for having to deal with an abuser who was going to get to keep her precious child without her around. She had a lawyer, but she wasn't very confident that they would be able to get full custody for her, as well as monitored visits with Alex. Since April had never called the cops and there weren't any police reports, a mistake on April's part, there was no proof that Alex would be unfit, so little chance of her getting full custody.

I guess Alex was biding his time and was going to try and win by getting as much custody of Joey as he possibly could. It's another way an abuser works. They hurt their partner by taking the child or children away.

I gave Aunt Carrie a hug good-bye when we returned home, and waved to April and Joey as she pulled her car up the driveway. Joey was sitting in her child seat in the back and waved enthusiastically at me when she saw me, giving me her biggest grin.

I went home in a good mood until, alone in my flat, I started thinking about Luke and wondered why he failed to tell me about how his family had died. If he really did trust me, why hadn't he told me about finding them murdered all those years ago? It's not something one would forget to mention.

Chapter 21

The next day it was late afternoon when we finally finished moving April and Joey. I was bushed. Aunt Carrie offered to feed me, but I begged off, needing rest more than I needed food.

It had been a long day and a lot of it was me looking after Joey.

Whew, I had no idea how much energy a three-year-old had. She kept me running. I mean, literally running, since I was fearful that she'd run out into the street. I had brought her up to my office for a distraction and a reprieve for me. She found the teddy bear I used to help my adult clients connect with their inner child. It was a rather strange looking, cockeyed teddy, but she loved it and took total possession of it. I didn't have the heart to make her leave it with me when she left, but her mother did.

I told April that it was okay if Joey kept the bear, but her mother insisted she give it back even with Joey screaming her displeasure. I finally took the bear and had the bear talk to Joey, telling her that it would be in MJ's house waiting for her to visit whenever she wanted.

That seemed to satisfy her, and being exhausted, her mother carried her back to Aunt Carrie's house. I felt a warm pleasure watching them go and felt like I had more family now that they were living next door. It made me smile, and I forgot about Jesse until I saw him walking up my driveway, picking his way through the construction debris toward my office.

What the hell is he doing here?

I rushed to the bathroom, splashed water on my face and combed my hair, trying not to look like I'd just spent the day hauling boxes and running after a three-year- old.

By the time I finished in the bathroom, I heard a knock on my door and went to open it.

"MJ, you didn't even ask who it was. I could have been anyone, and why don't you have an alarm, or at the very least a peephole so you can see who's outside your door?"

Jesse's a cop; he thinks in terms of criminals, murder, and rape. I don't blame him for his concern, but I did see him coming toward my place and it was a pretty good assumption that whoever was knocking at my door was him.

When I explained this to him, he asked if he could come in. I ushered him in and offered him the sofa as I took my therapist chair across from him.

"Why are you here?"

I wasn't going to make it easy for him. I also didn't want to show any vulnerability and acted like it didn't matter and that he was kind of an annoyance for showing up unexpectedly. If I were to analyze my behavior, I would have said that I was protecting and defending myself from getting hurt. And, if I were really honest, I wanted him to hurt the way I was hurting.

"MJ, I. . ."

I just looked at him and waited. I have to admit, I wanted to see him squirm a little bit. Something was up, and I knew we wouldn't be dating or having wild sex any time soon.

"Okay, look, I'm sorry about reneging today. I could have figured out a way to come, but I just didn't want to have to face you."

The look on my face must have shown surprise and confusion because he hurriedly went on. "This is difficult for me to say."

"Jesse, just say it already, okay? You can't see me anymore for some reason right? There, was that so hard?"

"MJ, I really like you. You are one of the bravest, most interesting, intelligent women I've ever met, and you're sexy as hell. . ."

Sexy, me sexy?

"But?"

"My wife came to me last week and wants to try again."

That was the last thing I expected to hear and all I could do was sit and stare at him.

"I have to try. It's the kids. If I don't try, I'll forever feel like I've abandoned them, and they'll feel it too. I can't do that to them. I've already spent way too much time on the job, neglecting them and their mother. I spent all those weeks after getting shot contemplating my life and my regrets about the kids, so when Jenny came to me last week and asked to try again, I had to say yes."

I couldn't look at him anymore because I felt tears come to my eyes. The thing was that I understood what he was saying. He was trying to do the right thing for his kids. How could I deny that? In fact, it made me like him even more than I already did.

"MJ, I didn't mean to lead you on. I really thought something nice could have happened between us.

Something nice *was* happening between us. I never in the world would have wanted to hurt you, and I'm so sorry."

As he reached out to me, I pulled back, stood up and said, "I think you'd better go."

He stood too, but didn't leave. I felt him approach me, but there was no place for me to go as I was up against my therapist chair. I felt him turn me toward him and put his arms around me to hold me tight. I couldn't stop myself and before I knew it, I was crying into his broad shoulders. It all seemed so unfair.

We stood like that for some time until I heaved a big sigh and started to push him away, not daring to look into his eyes from embarrassment.

Head down and turned away from him, I asked him to go. When he didn't make a move to leave, I said, "Now, please."

Chapter 22

Franny has always been my go-to person for personal relationships. We have spent hours and hours discussing boyfriends and spouses, both the good and the bad. I needed Franny after Jesse left.

"He's going back to his wife," I said into the phone.

"No way."

"Yup. He is. And I never saw that coming. It seemed like they were so over. She was in a very strong relationship with another man. She was even living with the guy. How did this happen?"

"MJ, something must have happened. You don't just kick your lover out one day and go back to your ex, just like that. I wonder what happened. Did Jesse indicate that he was seeing her at all over the past six months or so?"

"No. But we never really talked about her. We talked about his kids and how guilty he felt about not spending more time with them, or taking better care of them."

"But nothing about his wife, right? Weren't they getting a divorce?"

"I'm not crystal clear about the divorce. She had asked him for it and I thought they were hammering out the details. She was in a hurry because of this other guy she was living with, so I don't know what happened."

"Do you want to know?"

"Franny, this was such a new thing with Jesse. It's not like we've even slept together yet. We were just dipping our toes in. I don't think I even have the right to get answers from him, you know?"

"I do know, but I, for one, would still like to know what happened."

A sudden thought occurred to me and I speculated, "I do know that his wife hated the fact that he was a cop out on the streets. She worried about him getting shot, or hearing he'd been killed. Jesse told me that she just couldn't take it anymore and wanted out. She spent many nights alone and he wasn't very good at communicating with her when he was at work, so she never knew what was going on. Maybe the fact that he's on a desk job now is making her feel safe."

"Maybe, but he's going back to active duty, isn't he? You told me that's all he talks about; that he can't stand sitting at a desk."

"I thought so, but he hasn't really talked about that for a while. Maybe not. Maybe he's permanently disabled and won't be able to pass the physical requirements, so she feels he'll be safe on the desk."

Franny agreed that it sounded like the most logical reason she was going back to Jesse, but it didn't make me feel any better.

My heart hurt, but it wasn't broken and I decided that I'd throw myself into my work and pay more attention to my remodel. After all, I did have a full life.

Franny wished me a good night and we ended our call, her telling me that she loved me and we'd plan a weekend trip together soon, her treat. It did give me something to look forward to.

I pulled out my sofa-bed and plunked my pillow down, expecting to open my iPad and watch a funny sitcom. But instead I just laid on my back and starred at the ceiling. I couldn't get that last passionate exchange between Jesse and me out of my mind. I'd never felt this kind of passion before, even with Gideon.

With that thought, I felt guilty and tried to shift my thoughts onto something else. I must have dosed off because the next thing I remembered is hearing a soft, little knock on my door.

It was light out already and my watch said 6:30 a.m. I wondered who in the world would be outside of my door this early, but the thought that it might be Jesse coming back and apologizing and declaring his undying love for me had me jumping up and hurrying to the door.

Remembering his warning the night before, I put my ear to the door and said, "Who is it?"

"It's me." It was said so softly, I could hardly hear it, and then realized it must be little Joey.

I opened the door and there was the little curly haired blond child, still in her pink kitty pajamas, looking up at me.

I knelt down beside her and said, "Joey, how did you get up here? Did you come over here all by yourself?"

I looked behind her and down the steps to see if her mother had been with her, but the steps were empty. I picked her up and carried her over to my sofa-bed and put her down as she chatted away, telling me she was a big girl and came by herself because I had told her she could visit my teddy bear any time she wanted.

As she looked up at me with her big blue expectant eyes, my heart melted and I wanted to squeeze her close to me, but didn't want to scare her. We hadn't known each other but for a few days and I wanted her to feel safe with me, so I looked around and saw the cockeyed bear stuck on one of my shelves, went over, picked him up and brought him back to Joey.

"Here you go, my little one."

She held him tight against her chest and said, "I've missed you so much, Lucy."

Oh, so he wasn't a he, after all, and she'd already named her Lucy.

Joey immediately started talking to Lucy and answering back for her, engaged in a full-on conversation that didn't include me, so I picked up my phone and called Aunt Carrie. I guess I needed to get April's phone number too, if this was going to be a repeat event.

It turned out that Aunt Carrie and April were both still in bed and didn't even know Joey was gone. I told them to not worry, she was fine with me, that I'd let her play a bit and then bring her back. However, I did wonder if they had locked their doors, or if Joey somehow figured out how to unlock them. I tucked that question away to ask them later. I did not want her wandering around this neighborhood all by herself, and if she was that good of an escape artist, they needed to figure out a way to contain her.

I was not a mother, but I was a worrier and often times imagined horrible things that could happen in the future. It caused me a lot of anxiety, especially after I almost got killed six months ago when Detective Slatter, aka Mike Rimichi tried to choke me to keep me from exposing his illegal drug racket.

As Joey played, I made myself a cup of coffee and then sat on my therapist chair and watched her enact an entire drama with Lucy. *What an imagination!*

When I finished my coffee, I picked her up, bear and all, and carried her back to her house, saying that Lucy officially belonged with them. She was weird looking anyway, with eye's that looked a bit crossed. I had bought the bear online and when it came with the funny eyes, I kept it, believing that my clients could relate more to imperfection. I know I did.

Joey was such a sweet little thing. My eyes watered as I walked back to my lonely apartment knowing I'd never have the experience of having my own child. After Jesse's rejection, I allowed myself to doubt I'd even have the experience ever again of having a partner.

I had to consciously shift my thoughts away from those emotional pains. Instead, I mentally went over what I had to accomplish that day. With Luke on the 5150 hold, I was able to relax, knowing he was some place safe. My other clients were relatively easy compared to Luke.

I did not want to think about Luke, but as I constructed my day, he kept popping up in my mind as a puzzle of which I did not have all the pieces.

Chapter 23

The construction noise was ear piercing, so I took my hearing aids out to dull the noise. There are some good reasons to be grateful for being hard of hearing, like not hearing crying babies on an airplane, or blocking out construction noises.

After plugging in my earbuds and listening to soothing music on my cell phone, I tackled some bills and went over my numerous emails. Soon I got sleepy and took a nap.

My buzzing phone woke me and I saw there was a text from Dr. Holden. She told me that Luke was doing well and that he now had his cell phone back from the police. He had left it at the murder scene and the police had kept it until they got everything they needed from it. Giving his cell phone back sounded like he wasn't a suspect anymore, but I didn't know police procedure.

Dr. Holden suggested that I call Luke and make an appointment with him for the next week. He'd be out of the 5150 hold and would be starting an out patient treatment program for PTSD at the Santa Monica Service Clinic by the end of the week. She told me that making an appointment with Luke for the next week was vital for his recovery.

Then she told me to give her a call later in the afternoon sometime after 4 p.m. when she'd be charting and winding down for the day. There was something she had to discuss with me.

I wondered what it could be. Maybe the police had something they shared with her? Anyway, I had a couple of hours yet, so I got up, stretched and put my walking shoes on. I needed to get outside for some fresh air and exercise. Maybe that would wake me up so I could get some work done. I felt so groggy and lacked any kind of motivation.

***

When 4 p.m. finally rolled around, I made the call to Dr. Holden, eager to hear what she had to say.

She told me that Luke was doing remarkably well, that he was taking his treatment seriously and cooperating with his medication.

When she hesitated, I asked if there was more.

"It's his family. His father and brother have remained in town and want to see him. I've recommended that he not see any family or friends until he's been stabilized, but they were quite insistent, so I let them visit with supervision."

"How did that go?"

"Not that good actually."

"What happened?"

"I was not there, and I was assured that nothing terrible happened. However, after the visit, Luke became withdrawn, went to his room, and wouldn't come out for dinner. I'm going to talk to him about this when I see him tomorrow, but I'm going to restrict visitors again. I think we all need to focus on what's going on with that family. Something is not right there."

"Yes, I agree. Thanks for the input. I appreciate it. Will you be following up on him when he gets outpatient treatment at the Clinic?"

She assured me she would be and I was happy about that. I liked Dr. Holden. She didn't hold back and freely shared her assessments with me and I assumed she would do the same with the clinic Luke was going to.

It was clear that the clinic would be treating him for PTSD, Dr. Holden would be monitoring his medication and overall treatment, and I would be working with Luke about his relationships with friends and family — especially family.

I also felt that I needed to know more about what happened in New Orleans and why Luke hadn't mentioned those murders to me when he first came to see me. Even after he found his roommates murdered, he still hadn't mentioned them to me. It seemed like that would be the first thing a client would want to tell his new therapist. What would be more important in someone's life than the murder of your entire family?

My intuition told me that there was more to this story and I wondered what it was.

I also thought about Otto and Aaron Haas and what they might be after. It seemed odd that they were so intent on taking Luke home with them since they had so little to do with him, and Luke didn't seem to want anything to do with them. What was the story between them anyway? Were they afraid that Luke would say something or reveal something about them that they did not want revealed? But what could that be?

There was much I did not know concerning Luke, but I do love a challenge and this was a challenge. I just hoped I was up to it. Knowing that I had a psychiatrist on my side made it seem less difficult because at least I had someone to consult with.

I looked up Luke's number on my cell phone and gave him a call, expecting it to go into voicemail, and was surprised when he answered.

"Hi, Luke, MJ Lange here."

"Hi, Dr. Lange."

"Dr. Holden just gave me a call and suggested that I set up an appointment for you for next week. I hear you're doing pretty well and that you'll be starting treatment for PTSD at Santa Monica Service Clinic later this week."

"Yes ma'am, yes I am."

"So, Luke, how are you really doing? In your words."

I heard him take a deep breath and let it out slowly before he spoke.

"I feel safe here, Dr. Lange. I am scared about going back home. I don't want to see all that mess."

It was interesting that he called all the blood a mess, but then again, he hated his roommates smoking in the house and leaving messes. He was a bit OCD about his surroundings and his personal grooming so it made sense he'd think of it as a mess that had to be dealt with.

"Of course you don't, Luke. Have the police been able to talk to you?" I realized this was a question I should have asked Dr. Holden. Plus, I had no idea who cleaned up after a murder like that. It didn't feel right for Luke to go back to his home when there was still blood all over the place. I'd have to find that out.

Luke told me that the only people he's seen outside of the staff and Dr. Holden were his father and brother. I didn't ask how that went because we were on a short phone call to set an appointment and I felt it would be wrong to bring up anything emotional over the phone.

We ended the call after setting the appointment, and then I called Jesse. I needed information: who cleans up after a murder? That was my excuse to talk with him. At the time, it seemed like a good reason for a call.

Surely, it seemed, Luke wouldn't have to clean the blood, but I didn't know. As his therapist, I needed to know just how much more trauma Luke was going to have to go through, but I could have gotten that information easily via the internet or calling the detective.

Jesse was kind and polite and informed me that it was the responsibility of the owner/landlord to clean up the place and that there were companies who did this kind of thing professionally in order to make sure it was done up to code.

Keeping it professional, I thanked Jesse and was about to say good-bye when he stopped me by saying my name. It was said like a question. I broke the connection and hung up, pretending that I hadn't heard him. I was a little embarrassed that I used this as an excuse to talk to him. Even though I was alone, I felt the flush of shame flash up from my neck to my cheeks and was glad I hung up so quickly.

I was relieved that Luke wouldn't have to clean the murder area. But even though it wouldn't be his job, he'd still have to decide if he could go back and live where the murders took place. I didn't see how he could do that. I know I wouldn't have been able to.

Chapter 24

The week seemed to fly by and I was happy to see my practice grow by two more clients. I knew that I was back in the game and it felt good to be working again. As much as I didn't like to admit it, Franny was right: I do better when I'm helping people.

Dr. Holden told me that Luke was back living in his house after all the evidence of the murders had been cleared and cleaned. He had assured her that he would be able to handle living there either alone, or with more roommates.

As to the roommates belongings, they were gone too. Their families had come to pack up their things and the landlord had had the entire place cleaned and shining by the time Luke got back home. He had returned to work at the beginning of the week and seemed to be handling everything well, which kind of amazed me. He had seemed so fragile the last time I had seen him in the hospital. Was this a flight into mental health on his part? In other words, was there a temporary disappearance of symptoms? Was there a part of him that needed to deny all the trauma he went through in order to stop having to really look at how these murders had affected him?

I was a little nervous about seeing him, but I also knew that he had been getting a lot of treatment from both the clinic and Dr. Holden.

I wasn't a trained trauma therapist, but I did know enough about trauma to know that I should not push him, which could be more traumatizing for him than helpful. The trauma treatment he was getting at the center would be dealing more with his reaction to the murders and what exactly happened. I was to be more of a support to his PTSD treatment, and be available to help him navigate his everyday life, like his job, his friends, and his family.

I must admit, I was very curious as to what he witnessed, both of the murder of his roommates and the murder of his family. My imagination was probably worse than the actual scene. I just remembered how horrible it was for me to walk in on my father's suicide. I can still see and feel what that was like, even though it had been decades.

***

When I opened the door for Luke to come into the room, he flashed me that dazzling smile he had the first time we met. He looked great: well fed, physically fit, happy.

I was kind of shocked at how good he looked. I had to be careful that I was not projecting my own past trauma feelings onto him.

After he was comfortably seated on the sofa, I picked up my notepad and pen and said, "It's good to see you, Luke. You look so much better than the last time I saw you."

"Thank you, Ma'am. I feel good being back home and working again. I'm back to my old routine."

"Are you taking the medications that Dr. Holden prescribed for you?"

"No, I stopped taking them when I got out of the hospital. They made me feel groggy and tired. I didn't feel like myself, so I stopped."

Oh dear, that wasn't what I had expected to hear. "Does Dr. Holden know this?"

"I think so."

I was concerned that he stopped taking them abruptly, but then I realized he was only in the hospital for three or four days and there wouldn't have been enough time for the medication to build up in his system to where quitting suddenly would be a danger. But I was still concerned that he just stopped taking them. Many of my clients would stop taking their medications because they didn't like the way the medication made them feel, but Luke had undergone a huge re-traumatization and in those cases, medication would be very helpful. I made a note to query Dr. Holden about this.

"So, Luke, tell me how you're feeling? How is it being back in your house?"

"Dr. Lange, I just feel relieved that Sahara and Joy aren't there any more. I was so stressed worrying about them messing up the place, smoking marijuana and stinking up my house. Also, I don't have to worry about strangers coming into my house and partying. I can find better roommates."

It was a bit disconcerting to hear him talk so simply about what happened. I was expecting more drama. I had thought he might be feeling some guilt or sadness, or even some fear about it happening to him too, since they hadn't caught the murderer.

But he didn't talk about any of those things. He seemed relaxed and happy that things were supposedly back to normal. Again, I thought maybe there was some kind of autism, or learning disability. It just wasn't normal, how he was acting.

I wasn't sure where to go with this, since he wasn't bringing up the present or past murders he happened upon, so I let him decide where he wanted to go in the session.

"What can I help you with today, Luke?"

"Well, the thing that bothers me is at work."

"What's happening at work?"

"Everyone keeps asking me what happened and I don't want to talk to them about it. It reminds me of the time after my family died and I'd tell people what happened."

I was extremely aware that Luke never revealed anything to me about the murders of his family, so I decided to tread lightly.

"How would people react when you told them about your family in New Orleans?"

"They'd treat me differently."

"How so?"

"It felt like they didn't want anything to do with me. We'd be getting along fine, but after I'd tell them about what happened, they looked at me funny. They'd back away and no one would want to get together with me after they heard.

"I can't imagine how that must have felt."

"It hurt, Dr. Lange. Hurt a lot."

His tone of voice sounded more like a child than an adult as he slumped down in the sofa.

I decided that it might be a good idea to have an educational psychologist do some testing to see if he had an undiagnosed learning disability. Or maybe, as I suspected before, he was on the autistic spectrum.

I told Luke that I would like to get a bit more background information from him since I hadn't gotten the chance before, and proceeded to ask him about his earlier life.

He told me that he had had trouble in school, but when he got into high school and excelled in football, things changed for him. The coach got him a tutor to help him pass his classes and he started to feel better about himself. He said he could read, but it had always been a struggle in elementary school. He denied ever being tested and said that his mother hadn't really paid much attention to his grades.

When asked about friends, he said that he didn't have any and kids made fun of him.

"Why did they make fun of you, Luke?"

"Well, for one thing, they'd tease me about my mama when she'd come to pick me up."

"Why did they tease you about your mother?"

"Well, my mama dressed like a hooker. She wore short skirts and tops that showed a lot of her breasts."

"How did that make you feel when she'd dress like that in front of other kids?"

"I didn't understand it at first because it was just my mama. When I was little, I cried for her because she wasn't around much. When I got older I knew that she dressed that way because she was drunk or high and hanging with a bad crowd. She had no pride in dressing right or taking care of her body."

"So maybe that's why it's so important to you to treat your body like a temple and why you can't tolerate it when other people, like your roommates, use drugs and don't treat their bodies right."

I was trying to help him link his negative feelings about his roommates to how he felt about his mother as a child. He didn't seem to have much insight of how old patterns and how his treatment as a young child might have something to do with how he managed his adult life.

He ignored what I said and continued on as if I hadn't said anything. "Later on her drug use got worse when Sam moved in."

"Sam was her boyfriend?"

"Yeah, he started living with us when I was in middle school."

"It must have been difficult for you without any support at home."

"I didn't know it could be any different, Dr. Lange. It was just the way it was."

At this point, I reminded him that he could call me MJ, that I wasn't a medical doctor and it was fine to use the name everyone else called me.

"Okay."

As I asked him more questions about his growing up years in New Orleans, I could tell he was getting more and more uncomfortable, so as the end of the hour approached, I brought the topic back to something more neutral.

"Luke, I'm glad that you are feeling comfortable in your house now and hope you continue to do so. As you know, I will be in contact with Dr. Holden to follow your trauma therapy. Is there anything you'd like me to discuss with her before our next meeting?"

"I like Dr. Holden. She's nice. I don't know about that guy at the clinic. I guess he's okay. I've only seen him one time, but I see him again tomorrow. I go there two times a week."

"Well, remember, you can always call Dr. Holden or me in between sessions if you need to. I know it's a lot of appointments for you to be going to right now, but we all want to make sure that you are recovering all right. You have had a big trauma finding your roommates murdered like that."

I almost included his past trauma in New Orleans, but he still hadn't discussed it with me. I was getting more and more intrigued as to why he hadn't.

We concluded with a reminder of our next appointment, which I wrote on the back of my business card and handed it to him.

After he left and I was making my professional notes, I decided that getting him tested would be a priority. I had some experience in testing, but it wasn't my focus. It would be better if someone who had a background in educational psychology could do the testing. Someone who was familiar with things like learning disabilities, ADHD, and autism. I'd give Dr. Holden a call to discuss.

I wasn't sure what I was dealing with and wanted to run a few things by Dr. Holden. I was concerned that Luke was not taking his medication and that he seemed so calm about the murder traumas. I left her a message to call me.

I had an uneasy feeling. Okay, call it an intuitive gut feeling that something wasn't right in the land of Luke. How could someone who came upon their roommates slaughtered, go back to the same house and feel relieved? How could they just go back to work and seem to have no visible negative after-effects?

Chapter 25

I wasn't surprised that Dr. Holden didn't get back to me right away, but when I felt my cell phone vibrate, I assumed it was her and I answered quickly. Too late I realized it wasn't Dr. Holden and the person calling was not someone I had wanted to talk to.

"So you're alive," the familiar voice boomed out at me.

"Hey, Al. Yup, alive and. . . . "

I was going to say, alive and well, but that wasn't exactly true. I was sad and a bit angry. Actually, I wasn't sure what I was feeling. Maybe a little bit betrayed by Jesse. Sure, he had to try with his kids, but if he didn't love his wife, why get back with her? Couldn't he spend time with his kids even if he was divorced?

"What's going on, MJ? I haven't seen you at a meeting for a while and you haven't even called me. As your sponsor, I thought I'd at least get a phone call."

"You're my sponsor? I thought you told me that I didn't have to admit I was an alcoholic?"

He laughed at that and I could just see him throw his head back as he roared his loud guffaw.

"You got me on that one, MJ. I'd love to see you at a meeting though. How about tomorrow morning?"

Ugh, I did not want to be going to an AA meeting. I hadn't had a drink all week long, even with Jesse breaking his terrible news to me. If I could go a week, didn't that mean I wasn't an alcoholic? Seems like I only drank out of grief. I didn't need to drink every day and I could stop any time I wanted.

"Are you still there, MJ?"

"Yeah, I'm here."

There was a pause; neither of us spoke and that part of me that protects myself from feeling anything and from getting too close to anyone said, "Could you just maybe leave me alone for a while?"

"Okay, MJ, I get it. Keep in touch. Don't be a stranger. Maybe come by sometime and we'll have a coffee together."

"Yeah, sure. Okay."

I was mumbling by this point and felt like a heel. Big Al was great. I liked him. I'd love to have coffee with him.

I'd love to have him for a friend, but it's that dang AA stuff he keeps throwing at me.

But another part of me said, "He's not throwing anything at you. It was a friendly call. He just asked to have coffee with you. It was you who added most of the AA stuff. Why do you always sabotage yourself? You could use another friend right now, someone to talk to, call him back and apologize."

But I didn't. I felt too self-protected. I knew I'd tell him stuff that wasn't mine to tell and that he'd have a logical and sane answer for me concerning Jesse, but I didn't want logical and sane. I wanted to bemoan the fact that Jesse was moving on without me. I wanted to sink into self-pity, feel sorry for myself, even have a shot of vodka. And that's just what I did later that night.

Darn it, why did Big Al have to call and ruin everything for me? I was running fast and furiously into my workaholism, denying that I was running.

I was pretty wasted by the time Dr. Holden got back to me, so I let her call go to voicemail and I did what I always do when I start drinking. I poured myself another shot.

***

When I came back to consciousness around 2 a.m., I was lying on my sofa bed, fully dressed, having no memory of making up the bed. I got up slowly, went to the sink and drank a ton of water until my thirst was quenched. In the bathroom, I brushed my teeth and washed my face. Looking in the mirror, I mumbled to myself, "Shit, maybe you *are* an alcoholic."

Wandering around my small space, I felt antsy and wasn't sure what to do. Old memories and more recent ones filled my head and I felt like I was going to jump out of my skin.

It was only 2:30 a.m. and I knew I wasn't going to sleep anymore that night, so I sat at my desk and began writing down what was bothering me about Luke.

After I wrote several pages, I realized that I wasn't writing about Luke at all, but about my past traumas. Once again, I had taken on a client that triggered my past.

I shook my head and made a list of what needed to be done for Luke.

First, I needed to ask Dr. Holden about his medication and if the clinic did testing. Then, I needed to recommend he get tested, either by the clinic, or some other private party.

I also really needed to find out more about his father and half-brother. I didn't think I could make progress with him if we couldn't either include them in the sessions, or at least have him open up about his time with them.

There was also something else that had been bothering me and at 2:30 a.m., it came to me. The police hadn't questioned me, and I had no idea if they had questioned Luke. I had no idea who may have committed these murders and it seemed strange that Luke wasn't more concerned about who might have done this. He was living in the house where the murders took place.

Why wasn't he either scared about the murderer coming back and killing him too, thinking he might be involved with whatever it was the roommates were involved with, or at the very least, why wasn't he anxious about living in the house where this had happened?

Maybe I was being too soft on Luke. Maybe I needed to push a little harder. I'd talk to Dr. Holden about all of this. I was anxious for morning to come, so I could call her back.

Chapter 26

When morning finally rolled around, I decided that I'd go to Big Al's AA meeting after all. I mean, I drank myself to unconsciousness without blinking an eye. I knew that wasn't what normal people did when they drank. But denial is a powerful force.

I felt ashamed and didn't look forward to admitting to Big Al what I had done, but I didn't see any other way around it. If I were going to be honest with him, that started with me being honest with myself — something I wasn't very good at.

The meeting went by in a blur. I can't say that I even heard a word; I was too embarrassed to talk to Big Al and was trying to think of a way out. I had gotten there after the meeting started and kept my eyes down in order to not make eye contact with him.

I had been worried for nothing; he didn't even come up to me and I left without talking to him. I didn't know if I owed him an apology for the way I had acted the day before, but I realized that I was left feeling bereft. I had wanted him to talk to me, to put his big hands on my shoulders and reassure me that I was going to be okay. Instead, I was left with a feeling of intense loneliness such that I hadn't experienced since Gideon first died.

***

When I got back to my place, I decided to stop in to see Aunt Carrie. We hadn't seen much of each other since April and Joey moved in a few weeks before and I missed her. I was sure seeing her would take away that horrible feeling of loneliness.

But Aunt Carrie wasn't home, and neither were April and Joey. Playing with Joey always brightened my day and I was hoping to become close friends with April.

I called Franny, but got her voicemail. I wanted to call Jesse so badly, but restrained myself. I was not a home wrecker and I should have never started with Jesse since he wasn't divorced yet. I knew better. It was my own fault. How many times have I counseled women to not get involved with a married man until they see the divorce papers.

With no one else to commiserate with, I called Dr. Holden back, even though I really didn't want to be dealing at the moment with all the issues that Luke had.

I was surprised when she answered. I put my professional hat on and we started to discuss Luke. She told me that she would try to get him to take the medicine she prescribed, but there was nothing she could do if he didn't comply. I knew that, and if he continued to refuse to take the medication, we'd have to work around it.

She then gave me the name and number of an educational psychologist who specialized in testing for ADHD and learning disabilities. After discussing it, we both agreed that according to the DSM-5 — the American Psychiatric Association's manual for Diagnostic Criteria — Luke would not be diagnosed with Autism Spectrum Disorder, which includes what used to be called Aspergers. However, we both agreed that there was something amiss in Luke's social interactions and we thought the testing could help us pinpoint what that was. And, there was also his obsession with cleanliness.

We hung up and I was left again with my own thoughts and feelings. I have to be honest and admit my first thought was that a shot of vodka would be just the thing that I needed to stop the emotions and thoughts that were whirling around in my head.

I put on my sneakers and went out for a walk, thinking the physical movement would help. Instead, it only made me more agitated. It felt like my head was going to explode.

I went back home and called Big Al.

He answered.

We spoke for a good thirty minutes when he finally told me to find an AA meeting and get myself to it. This was the last thing I wanted to do, but I was so agitated that I did what he said.

He also told me that I was to come to his morning meetings, which were three times a week, and the next day I was to get up early in order to find pastries to bring to the group.

After we hung up, I went on line and found a meeting at a church in Santa Monica and a nearby pastry shop.

Homework done, I was overcome by extreme fatigue and decided to take a short nap until the Santa Monica meeting.

I fell asleep and missed the meeting entirely. I stayed in bed, sleeping fitfully and waking several times with nightmares of trying unsuccessfully to wash all the blood off of the walls.

Chapter 27

When Luke came for his next session, he was dressed casually in blue jeans and a t-shirt, with a gray sweat shirt draped over his shoulders. I could tell he took great pride in how he looked by the clothing he wore. He gave me his million dollar dazzling grin and sat comfortably on the loveseat sofa.

After handing him the paper with the name and number of the educational psychologist, I told him that to better treat him, I'd like him to go in for some testing. I told him that his comment about not doing very well in school may indicate that he had some kind of learning disability and it might be a good idea for him to get tested.

"Sure, Dr. Lange."

He ignored my wishes for him to call me MJ, so I decided to ignore it too.

"Is your family still in town, Luke?"

I wasn't prepared for the dark shadow that passed over Luke's face as he lost his grin, frowned and said, "Yes, ma'am. They are."

"You don't seem to be so happy about that. Is that true?"

"I don't know why they're here. My father never gave a care about me all those years growing up. Why should he care now?"

"But didn't your brother and your father ask you to live with them after your family in New Orleans were killed?"

There, I used the word "killed" and wondered if he'd comment on that, but he seemed to ignore it and said instead, "That's right. They felt guilty and had me come to California to live with them, but all they did was argue and fight over me."

"Over you?"

"I heard them more than once arguing about me."

"What were they arguing about?"

"Aaron, he kept saying that Otto was a hypocrite, a racist. Why hadn't he brought me to live with them earlier."

"It sounds like Aaron was angry at your father."

"Biological father. He's not my real father. A real father is there watching you grow up. A real father comes to your football games, cheers you on, is proud of you."

"He wasn't there for you."

"That's right. You know, I got a trophy for best player my last two years in high school. There were scouts that came to watch me play my last year. They came to watch ME. They were going to offer me a football scholarship, even though I wasn't smart. They wanted me for football."

"Luke, that's great. Did they give you an offer?"

"No."

"Why not? What happened?"

"You want to know what happened? You want to know what happened?"

He was getting agitated and half rose from his chair as if to lunge at me. I couldn't help but gasp and shoved my chair back. I'd not seen this kind of aggression in Luke before and it scared me, but before I could react, he sat back down and told me what happened.

"It was my last football game. After playing four years of high school, it was my last football game. Since it was the last game, I begged my family to come. My mama, my Auntie, and Sam all promised they'd be there."

I had guessed what was coming and my heart reached out to him, even though I was still a bit frightened.

"After the game, there was an awards event at the school gym. I was honored as best player. It was an award sought after by all the players, but I won it."

He pounded on his chest once with his fist as he spoke of his win.

He then paused and looked up as if he were seeing the event in the distance and kept shaking his head slowly back and forth.

"You must have been so proud," I managed to say, noticing that he had disengaged with me. It seemed like he was actually seeing himself back as a teenager.

"When I went up and took the award, I looked out at all the parents and families, and the rest of the team. And you know what I saw?"

"No. What did you see?"

Ignoring me, he said, "I saw none of my family; not my mama, not my Auntie, and not Sam. And for sure I did not see Otto, but I wouldn't have known it if he was there anyway, since he never showed himself all those years of me growing up. I didn't even know what he looked like."

"Luke, I'm so very sorry. It must have been so disappointing for you."

"It was at that moment I decided to never play football again. I was through."

I could see the anger that was still boiling inside, but I also saw that hurt kid and wanted to put my arms around him and comfort him.

"What happened when you didn't see your family?"

He told me he thanked the team and then walked the five miles back home; alone, in the dark. At one point, he threw his trophy as far as he could throw into an empty field, knowing that if he didn't have family or anyone who cared enough to even come see him play, the trophy meant nothing to him either.

When he got home, all the lights were on in the house as if there was a party going on and he had a momentary hope that his family was waiting quietly to surprise him when he walked in the door. He had hoped that maybe they hadn't come to the game because they were making a big celebration for his achievement and wouldn't have had time to prepare if they had gone to the game.

He had chuckled to himself at the time and wished he hadn't thrown his trophy away and had decided he'd go back the next day and try to find it. He'd pretend he was surprised when they jumped out at him, congratulating him and making it a big deal.

But when he walked into the house through the kitchen door, no one jumped out at him. It was very quiet, he didn't even hear the tinny music from his mom's cell phone that was often playing as his mama and Sam would sway to the music in a drunken or drug-induced high.

He had called out to see if anyone was home. With all the lights on, he thought it strange when no one answered. After dropping his backpack on the kitchen floor, he walked into the dining room.

At this point in his narrative, Luke faltered in describing what he had seen. He just stared at me, then said in almost a whisper, "My mama, my auntie, and Sam were all lying on the floor and blood was everywhere. It was a terrible mess." He went on to explain that they were brutally murdered with what must have been a large knife or some kind of machete.

"They still don't know who did it. The police thought it had been some kind of revenge killing that had something to do with drugs. They really didn't spend much time on it, since the victims were all drug users too, and those kinds of murders were common around there. It became a cold case pretty early on. I try not to think about it."

Chapter 28

We sat together in total silence, Luke staring out the window with me trying to absorb what he had just told me.

I noticed that I had a tear running down my face, but Luke held on to his fierce rather detached look. It wasn't the murders that made me cry, for I had no sadness over the death of these people I had never met. It was the emotion of sadness and disappointment that I was feeling for Luke at the image of him walking the five-mile distance in the dark, alone, knowing that there was no one who cared about him.

How could a young man who was brought up by a drug addict, abandoned by his father, forced to figure things out on his own, end up being so polite and seemingly kind? His smile alone showed an inner light that shined out of his inner core.

When he finally turned to look at me, I was lost for words, and we stayed gazing at each other for a long time.

"Luke, I am lost for words."

"You see why I don't talk about this to people? They look at me funny after they hear the story. I can't stand to see that look in their eyes."

"Do you see that look in my eyes?"

He hesitated and cocked his head to one side and that bright, dazzling grin slowly started and he said, "No, no, I don't see it."

***

We made another appointment and Luke left. I sat and contemplated what he had just told me. I had to fight the urge to rage and blame his mother for the way she raised him, for not being there for him, and for getting herself in so much trouble that she ended up dead in some awful drug deal gone wrong.

I knew this was one of my defense mechanisms for not feeling the real sadness and emotional pain from what he told me about how dejected he felt when no one showed up for his final game. I had to shut it down so I wouldn't go down the dark hole of depression that his story triggered in me.

I don't tell people about how my father died either. The cloying sympathy people exude when I share the story makes me feel more alone — but not just alone; it makes me feel weak.

I understood Luke, but I also had to keep myself detached enough so I wouldn't be projecting all of my sadness and abandonment on to him.

I didn't know enough about his relationships with his family to judge, but there seemed to be an incongruity there; his politeness vs what one might expect from someone raised by a single mother who was also a drug addict. It was like a puzzle where the pieces weren't fitting together to form a complete picture and I didn't have the cover depicting what the puzzle was supposed to look like.

I needed to talk to that detective who had called me. I couldn't remember his name and if he had given me his card, I had no idea where I had put it. I figured Dr. Holden would know, so I called her and left a message for her to get back to me with his name and number.

I kept wondering what would be the odds of a similar murder happening in one's house, decades apart. Did someone have it in for Luke? Were these really just two separate events that had to do with some drug sale gone bad? Had they eliminated Luke as a suspect? What the hell was I dealing with?

If that happened to me twice, I'd be a basket case. You wouldn't get me moving back into my house. I didn't understand why no one, like Dr. Holden or the clinic he was going to for trauma, would allow Luke back in that house. Maybe they didn't have any control over it.

After writing some notes for the session, I couldn't sit still and decided to call Luke. I needed to talk to his father and brother. Maybe they could shed some light on what happened, or why Luke was acting the way he was.

He answered immediately, "Hey, Dr. Lange. Did I forget something?"

"No, Luke, you didn't forget anything, but I did forget to ask you about your father and brother."

"What about them?"

"Well, I was hoping they could come with you for the next session."

"Why?"

I didn't hear any upset in his voice, but his short answers didn't allow me to evaluate what he might be feeling.

"Well, for me to help you the most, I need to look under every rock, so to speak. There seems to be something going on between you and your father and brother, is that not true?"

I probably shouldn't have opened up a whole new discussion so soon after he disclosed what happened the night his family in New Orleans was murdered, but it came out before I had time to think.

"What I meant to say," I tried to remedy my mistake, "was that I think it would be beneficial for our work together if we had a session with your father and brother."

"Okay, Dr. Lange. You're the doctor."

I was a bit surprised that it was so easy to get him to agree so I quickly asked him if he could invite them to our next session. He agreed and that was that.

A text had come in while I was on the phone with Luke and I saw that Dr. Holden had left Detective Nordell's number for me, which I quickly called without hesitation.

He answered my call with a curt, "Detective Nordell."

"Detective Nordell, this is MJ Lange. I'm the psychologist who was with Luke Brown the day his roommates were murdered. Do you remember me?"

"What can I do for you, Ms. Lange?"

He did not show any kind of kindness or sympathy, just a rather cold demeanor.

"I was wondering if Luke has been eliminated as a suspect and if that's maybe why you haven't contacted me for an interview about the case?"

"As far as we can tell, Luke seems to be in the clear. The time factor alone would make it almost impossible for him to have been able to kill his roommates between the time he left work and the time he called 911. However, nothing's absolutely impossible, but we just don't see him as the killer. There's no evidence that he did it. We have no weapon, he didn't have any blood on his clothes, and he wouldn't have had the time to stash a weapon, or to change his clothes."

I let out a breath that I didn't even know I'd been holding. Had I honestly thought that Luke might be the murderer?

Thanking Detective Nordell, I was about to ask him if they had any leads, but he had already hung up on me.

Chapter 29

I spent the rest of the day trying to get Luke's story out of my head. It helped that I had two more clients scheduled for later, so I knew they would be a distraction.

Since I hadn't seen Aunt Carrie for what seemed like ages, I ran over, picking my way through the construction site, then through the gate and knocked on her back door. It was quiet and peaceful looking out over her garden. When she opened the door with a dish towel thrown over her shoulder, I saw flour on her arms and a white patch of it on her nose and I could smell yeast emanating from the kitchen table.

Joey was kneeling on a chair in front of an array of yeasted bread dough, her little fists punching the rising dough down. When she saw me, she grinned at me and said, "MJ, wook what I doing. I punching the bwead. We need to huwt it so it will get bigger again, wight gwamaw?

I laughed at her interpretation of hurting the bread in order for it to grow bigger. Since I was wearing black slacks and a black sweater, I chose a chair at the table that distanced myself from the flour storm taking place. It brought back fond memories of when I was a child and my paternal grandmother let me help make yeast bread. There was nothing like fresh warm baked bread coming out of her oven, on which I would slather butter and honey.

"What are you making? It smells so good. Will there be sweet rolls?"

"MJ, you have an uncanny ability to know exactly when my sweet rolls will come out of the oven. Pour yourself a cup of coffee; they'll be done in a few minutes."

It felt so safe and warm in the little 50s style kitchen and I really needed some comfort food.

While waiting for the sweet rolls to cool, I watched as Aunt Carrie and Joey finished shaping dinner rolls and then covered another batch of dough to sit on the sunny window ledge in order to rise. It was such a domestic scene, it took me away from murder and family discord and old emotional traumas. If only I had had a home like this one, maybe I wouldn't have turned into such a basket case.

I assumed that April was at work and that Aunt Carrie was babysitting Joey. I hadn't really spent much time with April, but I knew she was pretty distracted with what all was going on with Joey's father, Alex. I did not want to overwhelm her any more than necessary, so I kept my distance. I figured there would be time enough for us to get to know each other.

"Does she get to see A-l-e-x?" I spelled out his name, not wanting Joey to know who we were talking about.

"Joey, tell MJ who you saw yesterday?"

Joey's eyes immediately lost their sparkle as she delicately picked small handmade bites from her sweet roll.

"Who'd you see?"

"I saw Daddy."

And with that, she got off her chair and asked Aunt Carrie to help her wash the sticky off her hands.

Aunt Carrie and I exchanged a look that didn't need words. Obviously, Joey wasn't that excited about seeing her father. I felt sorry for Joey and April, and now Aunt Carrie who was thrown into the mix.

After Aunt Carried helped little Joey wash her hands, she told Joey to go play in the other room because she was going to clean up. That gave us a moment for talking without little ears hearing.

"What's going on with Alex and April?"

She didn't answer immediately, but took her fork and started eating the remains of Joey's left over sweet roll.

"Well, she has that restraining order keeping Alex away from her, but he does get to see his daughter every other week-end and Wednesday evenings. Last night was the first Wednesday Joey saw her dad since April kicked him out. April had to take her to the police station for the exchange due to the restraining order. It was a bit traumatic for everyone."

"Yeah, I can only imagine. It must be so hard for April to let Joey see him."

"It is, but that is the way the court set it up. There's not much to do about it and he is her father."

"Do you know if Alex has ever hurt Joey?"

"Not that I know of. April says that Alex mostly ignored her and left all the child care to April and then complained that April wasn't paying enough attention to him."

I knew this was a classic symptom of an abusive relationship, but kept my mouth shut. I was there to support Aunt Carrie and as much as I could, April and Joey. But I was't really involved, so I thought it best to just listen.

"Oh, MJ, I'm so glad my daughter and Joey are here with me. I hope I can keep them safe. I'm just glad April isn't married to Alex and they don't have to also go through a terrible divorce. I mean, it's hard enough for April to have to try to work things out with Alex through the court system."

I knew that the court had set up a temporary visitation schedule and that they were to work out a more permanent schedule after they had mediation. If mediation didn't work, then the judge would decide the fate of Joey. Such a cruel system, but I have no answer for a better one at the moment. When two people can't come to any agreement, or work together for the good of the child, it mostly sucks.

I felt sorry for all of them. It's not a good thing to be a part of the Family Court system, because I knew the judges had a lot of power there, and in a he said — she said scenario here in California, the judge usually gives an equal amount of time for each parent.

I just hoped that Alex didn't try to use Joey as a pawn to get back at April for leaving him, which often happened in cases like theirs.

I reached over and gave Aunt Carrie a hug and said, "Try not to worry too much about it. April and Alex will do what they do. Stay strong in your belief that April will find the way out of this situation that will be the best for both Joey and herself."

I was a fine one to talk. I'd never been able to not worry, but it doesn't keep me from suggesting it for someone else.

Since Joey was in the living room playing with her toys, I went to say bye-bye to her. She had set up a little tea party and Lucy Bear was part of the it. My heart warmed at finding I had a small part to play in her happy little event by letting her have the stuffed bear, wonky eyes and all. I was aware that I was starting to fall in love with this little girl.

Leaving their house, I stopped for a minute to talk to my contractor on my way home. It looked like things were coming along. I wasn't a very good judge of construction, so I decided to trust the guy. After all, Franny referred him to me and I knew he had done a lot of work on her Santa Monica home, and her house was fabulous.

Spending time with Aunt Carrie and Joey was a distraction, but as usual, the minute I was alone, all the questions start to pop up about Luke and his family and I wanted a drink badly. But I refrained and felt pretty good about myself. Once again, convincing myself that I wasn't an alcoholic.

Chapter 30

The week went by uneventfully. I saw my current clients and took on another new one. I was able to get the pastries to Big Al's AA meetings and because he had given me that job, I of course, had to be at the meetings. I knew that was Big Al's intention in the first place, but once I'm given a task and I agree to it, I feel responsible and can't let anyone down.

When Luke came in for his next session, he arrived alone. I was confused because I thought he had asked his father and brother to come.

"Don't worry, I asked them and they said they'd come. They're probably just trying to find a parking space. We didn't come together."

I had Luke sit on the loveseat and had put out two extra chairs so the four of us would form a circle. Luke would face me, and Otto and Aaron would sit across from each other.

I've done a lot of family sessions, but this one had me a bit worried. Usually, I have a better understanding of the family dynamics. This family seemed like they were holding a lot of secrets, so I had planned on acting more like an investigative journalist to find out what was going on.

As Luke and I exchanged pleasantries, we heard a loud knock on the door and I got up to let Otto and Aaron in. They were both over six feet tall and with their cowboy hats and boots, they towered over my short five-foot-three frame. They seemed to take up all the space in my small office and I struggled not to feel intimidated.

I indicated where they should sit and we all sat for a few minutes in awkward silence while they took their cowboy hats off and, in tandem, placed them on their knees.

"Well, I guess I should begin by first thanking you both for being here to help Luke deal with his traumas. What was it that got you both here today?"

"Luke asked us to come," Aaron said.

"And what was it he said that made you come?" I was addressing both of them, but knew Otto would not be participating much since he sat and folded his arms across his chest with a rather disagreeable look on his craggy face.

"Luke asked us to come and I'd do anything for Luke. I have no idea why he came," he said pointing his chin at his father.

"Why do you think I asked both of you to come, Aaron?"

"I imagine you want to know what the hell is going on in this family, and I have to say, I'd like to know the same thing."

I looked at Otto, who just glared at his son, refusing to make eye contact with me. Luke sat very still and did not look at anyone, so I decided to engage him as my co-therapist.

"Luke, why do you think I asked your family to come in today for your session?"

"Dr. Lange, I trust that you had a good reason to invite them, but I don't really know why you asked them. I don't see how they could help. Just being around them makes me nervous. I can feel the anger between them and it scares me."

I looked over at Otto to see how he might be taking this. It surprised me to see that the hard look on his face had softened a little after Luke spoke.

"Otto, may I call you Otto, or would you prefer Mr. Haas?"

"It makes no never mind to me, Dr. Lange."

"Please, call me MJ," I said hoping he would continue to soften up. I don't do well with hard-hearted people, especially men.

When I didn't get a response, I tried again, "Mr. Haas, why do you think Luke feels so nervous around the two of you?"

Aaron scoffed at that question and Otto looked at him with daggers in his eyes.

"There seems to be a lot of tension between you two," I said pointing at the two of them. "Would you mind sharing with me what that's all about?"

"Dr. Lange, I don't think that's any of your business, if you don't mind me saying," Otto said.

He spoke slowly in a way that seemed polite, but with an underlying hard edge.

"It isn't any of my business per se. I'm just trying to get a clue why Luke feels so uncomfortable around the two of you. Most people who've experienced a trauma such as Luke did, twice, need support from their family. This isn't about the two of you. But when both of you, from what I can see, can't seem to stand the sight of each other and are constantly bickering, I'd like to better understand what's going on. It might help Luke come out of this second set of murders in a more healthy state of mind. If you really want him to come live with you, but the two of you can't stand each other, how could that be helpful for Luke? Can you understand this?"

"Of course he can't understand this. He's never been able to understand emotions. All he understands is the bottom line. Money. Just ask my mother. He has no heart."

So much anger in Aaron toward his father. I wondered if it all come from seeing his mother as the victim of a terrible marriage and feeling powerless to do anything about it.

"Aaron thinks I caused his mother's MS."

"I remember it was mentioned before at the hospital. But what I want to know is how that belief impacts what Luke is experiencing at the present. And do you both really think Luke would be better living with you instead of living here in Los Angeles with his friends? Could either one of you even be able to put your differences aside in order to have Luke feel welcome in your homes? You both seem determined to have him come live with you. I'm wondering why?"

With that I turned toward Luke and asked him why he thought they were so determined for him to come live with them.

"They feel guilty. They aren't doing this for me, but to feel less guilty."

"Is that true?" I directed my question to the two men facing each other like two bulls.

"I don't feel guilty at all. He," he pointed at his father, "should feel very guilty."

"Why is that?"

"First of all, he leaves my mother to take care of me alone while he runs away to New Orleans and has an affair with Luke's mother. Then he comes back home expecting her to take him back, just like that, and to be a part of the family. But not just to be a part of the family, but also as the head of household, taking all control away from my mother. He thinks coming back to take responsibility for his family and the orchard was some kind of noble act, but what he really wanted was the orchards. The business is worth millions and he knew granddaddy would leave it directly to me if he didn't come back and eat crow. Isn't that right Otto?"

Otto just looked down at his hands and shrugged, but the displeasure on his face remained in place.

I thought I'd have more luck getting information out of Otto if I could see him alone. He didn't seem much like airing his dirty laundry in public, so I doubted I'd get much from him, but it felt like there was more to the discord between them than met the eye.

The rest of the session went downhill. Aaron continued to debase his father. Luke remained pretty quiet, and

Otto just glared at Aaron, but remained mostly quiet. This seemed incongruous to me because Otto didn't seem like the type of man who would sit and take this kind of put-down from his son.

I was left feeling pretty powerless and decided that it hadn't been such a good idea to have a family session with both Aaron and Otto. I didn't really learn anything new that could help Luke, but I did help facilitate an agreement that Luke would remain in Los Angeles and Otto and Aaron would stop demanding he come home with them.

We agreed that if they wanted to see Luke, they could invite him out for a meal or a sporting event and Luke would have the choice of saying yes or no. They weren't happy about it, but they both agreed this would be the prudent thing to do. I explained that Luke was having treatment for PTSD and didn't need a lot of added stress on his system right now and that maybe in the future, when he was doing better, we could all try again to see how Luke could be integrated into their family.

The session left me drained and even more confused than before. I felt even more strongly that this family was harboring some significant secrets.

Chapter 31

After the session with Luke's family, I really wanted to drink. A shot of vodka seemed like the quickest way to calm my mind. But I decided to call Big Al instead.

Not surprising, he told me to get to a meeting.

Instead, I called Franny and we met for an early dinner. I felt that three meetings a week were enough. I didn't mind going to the meetings with Big Al, but the other ones usually left me feeling bored and frustrated. I still hadn't shared at one, and wasn't about to, regardless of what Big Al suggested.

We met at Wally's in Santa Monica. It was a little more expensive than I liked, but without drinks, I felt it was doable. I ordered one of the cheaper things on the menu, the vegetable fettuccine, and Franny got the more expensive dish of King Salmon. I really, really wanted a glass of red wine to go with my fettuccine, but I refrained. Franny, on the other hand, had a chardonnay and I eyed it with lust as she took small sips from her elegant wine glass.

I couldn't understand how someone could just sip on their wine. Me, I would gulp it down and then order another.

She asked me how Luke was doing but I didn't want to discuss it, so changed the subject to Franny herself.

Of course, she was happy to oblige and talked endlessly about a few of the charities she was supporting, one of them a safe house for abused women.

The mention of the safe house caught my attention and I asked her where it was. She said that she didn't even know. It was kept a pretty big secret, so the abusers wouldn't be able to find their spouses or partner and their children.

I thought of April, but didn't think she was really in any danger at the moment. There was a restraining order and he'd obeyed it so far, but who knew how long that would last.

We talked about April, and Franny reminded me how a new break up is when it's the most dangerous for the victim.

I reacted to the term victim and we went round and round about semantics. I loved our conversations. They were usually stimulating and interesting on a whole host of topics. I had missed them when we had been estranged for two years after Franny had tried to become a relationship coach without getting any type of training. I had felt betrayed and she pushed ahead without listening to my concerns. But eventually we reunited and worked out our differences, once again becoming best friends and vowing to never let anything get between us again.

It felt good to me that I knew someone who had a connection with a safe house just in case April and Joey needed one. I had become attached to Joey and wouldn't want anything bad to happen to her or her mother.

I asked Franny if she was still carrying her little pistol around.

"You know, it's been a while since that guy threatened me, so I've kind of forgotten to put it in my purse."

I was relieved. I hated guns and did not approve of Franny having one, let alone carrying one, but it wasn't a deal breaker for me. If it made her feel safe, then it wasn't up to me to persuade her to get rid of it.

She had bought a small gun after one of her coaching clients had threatened her, accusing her of not handling a situation correctly. This is exactly why I was so angry at Franny for starting a relationship coaching business in the first place. I knew her personality and even though she's a natural when it comes to perception and reading people, she's not always very diplomatic and can get herself in hot water. Thus, her need to carry a gun to protect herself from a disgruntled coaching client.

We continued to gossip until Franny asked me about Jesse. I didn't want to talk about him either. Out of sight, out of mind was my motto. I was ashamed that I allowed myself to get hung up about a guy who wasn't yet divorced, so I didn't want to be reminded about it.

"Franny, I don't want to talk about it, okay?"

"Sure, okay. No problem. I just wanted to know if he was for sure going back to his wife."

When I started to protest, she held up her hand and said, "Hold on, hold on. The reason I asked was because I have someone I'd like to introduce you to."

"No way, Franny, not going to happen."

"Wait, you don't even know who it is or anything about him."

"I don't care. I'm not going on a blind date. I hate those things. Besides, I don't think I'm ready."

"You're still hung up on Jesse, aren't you?"

"No, of course not, don't be silly."

"Then, why don't you let me set you up? He's a nice man, very intelligent. And, he's rich too."

I looked at her and realized I wasn't going to win this one, but then I remembered something I heard at an AA meeting. I told her that it was suggested that we don't get into any relationships the first year we're in recovery. She was one of my best supporters for my sobriety and I knew she'd back off if I told her this.

"Okay, MJ, I hear you. We'll wait a year, but what if we just happened to be at the same place at the same time?"

I threw my hands up in the air and looked around for the waitress. It was time to end our chat. I was proud of myself for not ordering a glass of wine, but it was time to end the conversation with Franny.

As I drove home, I felt good. I hadn't had a drink and was able to deflect the conversation away from Jesse and Luke. However, as I got closer to my place, I didn't really want to go home and be alone. I knew I'd start ruminating about both of them and I could feel the anxiety I tried so hard to dampen, rising up in my guts.

Chapter 32

Once in my flat, I realized that I wanted to share with Big Al the fact that I didn't have a drink when I was out with Franny. I had a need for him to be proud of me. I guess he was becoming a father figure for me and wondered if that was a normal feeling to have for an AA sponsor.

I worried it was too late to call, that Big Al might already be in bed. He had to be in his late seventies and got up early every morning, so I assumed he went to bed early too.

However, when I saw who had called me while I was out enjoying myself, I decided to call him back after hearing his message. It wasn't Big Al.

He answered on the first ring.

"Mr. Haas, I know it's late, but your message sounded urgent. What's going on?"

"Dr. Lange, I've been stewing on this for a while and not sure I'm doing the right thing, but once I make up my mind, I rarely change it. I'm leaving Los Angeles and going back home tomorrow mornin'. I had hoped to bring Luke back with me, but I can see he's in good hands here with you and the rest of the team at that clinic there."

"Okay."

"Aaron is staying here. He has some kind of thinking going on in his head that Luke needs him. Ever since he found out he had a brother, he's been on some sort of hero's journey to save him, even if he doesn't need nor want saving."

I didn't think that needed a response and wondered where all this was going.

" You should know that Aaron was in New Orlean's when Luke's mother was murdered."

"Yeah, I think I knew that. What are you trying to say?"

"I'm not sure what I'm trying to say, but I need to get this off my chest. It's twisting my guts."

"Mr. Haas, you really haven't told me anything. I'm not sure what you're implying. Maybe you should just come right out and say what you're worried about."

"Aaron was also in Los Angeles when Luke's roommates were murdered."

I had to digest this new information a bit before I asked, "Are you worried that Aaron had something to do with both of the murders?"

There was nothing but silence at the other end. I guess if I had any doubts about a son of mine committing murder, I'd probably be speechless too.

"Have you said anything to the police?" I asked.

"Dr. Lange, what is it I'd say to them? My son might have killed all of those people? But with a knife? That would be a mighty intense thing to do, don't you think? Especially since he has a gun and a permit to own and carry one. Shooting someone would be a faster and cleaner way to do it, don't you think? I just can't see Aaron having that kind of passion that would murder a bunch of people with a knife. A gun would be more to his liking. And, I can't figure out what his motive would be."

"Okay, you're telling me this for a reason. You said you needed to get it off your chest. What is it you're really trying to say here, Mr. Haas?"

I heard a big sigh and waited patiently. He was either going to tell me, or he was going to make some excuse and back away from having shared and tell me it was a big mistake, that he was just being paranoid. I wouldn't blame him. Who would want to think his own son was capable of such an act?

"There's a part of Aaron that is still this sweet little boy who's looking for reassurance and ways to make me proud. I know I was a terrible father when he was young. I had no idea how to be a father. I didn't want to be like my own Pa, who was a mean son-of-a-bitch. His idea of teaching me anything was to throw me in the deep end and see if I sunk or swam. I tried not to do that with Aaron, but instead I mostly ignored him.

"Isabelle, his mother, tried to make up for my lack of attention, but she coddled him too much and made him soft. When she was diagnosed with MS, Aaron blamed me for it, saying I didn't pay enough attention to her." He stopped talking for a minute and then continued, "I don't know, maybe I did cause it."

Maybe it was the lateness of the hour, or maybe he had had a drink and was in a more mellow mood, but I would have never suspected him of divulging such humanness. I liked this Otto, and felt for him. The fact that he and Aaron were at such odds, that he would even consider questioning his son of such brutal murders must have been extremely difficult for him to admit even to himself, let alone a stranger.

"I hear you Otto, but you still haven't explained why you think that Aaron may have the capacity for such brutal murders."

"Huh, I guess I got side-tracked there. As I said, there is that part of him that really needed and still needs my attention and approval, but then there's the other side that is steeped in anger. More like rage, and I've seen him lose it a few times."

"Can you give me an example?"

"The worst time was when a worker screwed something up when we were putting in a new micro-sprinkler irrigation system. Aaron saw red and attacked the poor guy. Three of us had to pull him off. I thought he was going to kill him."

"So what happened then?"

"I had to pay the guy off to not report it. Then Aaron got angry at me for fixing it for him. I don't know, maybe I should have let him suffer the consequences. The one thing I thought I was doing right was fixing things for Aaron. Now, I think baling him out was maybe the worst possible thing I could have done."

Hearing what Otto had to say about Aaron didn't necessarily mean Aaron would kill a house full of people. It meant he had a temper that, when it got triggered, maybe he couldn't stop.

I wondered if something like that could have happened in New Orleans and wondered what could have set him off since he didn't even know those people. I guess happening upon people using drugs could have set him off, so the murder of the roommates could have been similar if they were also using drugs. It just seemed so far-fetched. When he wasn't raging at his father, I liked Aaron. He seemed to really care about Luke.

"Mr. Haas, what is it you think I might be able to help with here?"

Another long sigh, "I don't rightly know, Dr. Lange."

"If you honestly think there's some connection between Aaron and the murders, you have to tell the police," I told him.

When he didn't answer, I realized that maybe he thought I might be the one to tell them.

"Let me think about it, Dr. Lange, and I'll get back to you. I hope that with me not around, you can get what you need with just Aaron and Luke."

He then lowered his voice to where I could hardly hear him, even though I had my earbuds turned up to the highest volume. "Maybe I just needed someone to reassure me that Aaron couldn't have done it and it was all going to be all right."

I had no idea how to respond to that, since I couldn't reassure him that it was all going to be all right. I was just as confused as he was, so I kept silent.

"Okay then," and he hung up.

I felt sorry for him, and sorry that I couldn't help him feel better. As a therapist, I can often offer words of encouragement, but mostly the encouragement is to reassure that my clients have the knowledge and inner strength to find solutions for themselves. But I couldn't even do that for Otto. I consoled myself in believing that he just needed to vent and he chose me as the person to talk to.

I sat late into the night with many thought and emotions running through my mind and decided that I most likely was not going to be getting any sleep. I wanted a shot of vodka so badly that I literally sat on my hands. When I saw it was already 1:15 a.m., I knew it was really too late to call Big Al. Even though he told me to call him any time of the day or night, but I'm sure he didn't mean one in the morning.

Chapter 33

I wasn't sure how it happened, but I did fall asleep while sitting on my loveseat, and when I awakened, my neck hurt. Not just my neck, but my whole body. I couldn't wait to get to my AA meeting so I could talk to Big Al about all that had happened. I realized that he was probably the one person I could share everything with. After all, his nickname was 'The Priest".

He was like a priest taking confessions and never divulged anything that was ever told to him. That's how I met him in the first place. The murdered anonymous caller, Joe, whom I had befriended the prior year, was in his AA meetings and had given Big Al information that had finally shut down a dangerous illegal drug ring in Venice. Big Al had been trusted with this information which he was instructed to give to me if something happened to Joe. Big Al had kept it safe and remained outside of the legal system the entire time, so I knew I could trust him with my life.

Since I trusted him, I wondered why I didn't reach out to him more. Who am I kidding? I didn't reach out to him more because I knew he'd eventually convince me that I'm an alcoholic and then I'd have to take the AA meetings seriously. He'd probably have me work a program of sobriety and I wasn't ready for that.

After the meeting, when I asked him to talk, he told me he had somewhere he had to be but we could set up a time to talk. I was disappointed. I told him that I hadn't called him at 1:15 a.m. when I had really wanted to drink. I knew it was a manipulation to get him to stay longer and talk to me, but he saw right through it.

"MJ, let's get some coffee tonight and we'll talk."

"I can't drink coffee at night. I already have a hard time sleeping when I'm worked up. Coffee will send me through the roof."

He threw his big head back and laughed that hardy, loud laugh, but I couldn't be offended that he was laughing at me. I knew that was just a tactic of mine to try and get him to see me sooner than the evening. I didn't have any clients for the rest of the day and had no idea how I'd get through it without cogitating about either Luke, Aaron, or Otto, or worse yet, Jesse.

"Okay," I relented, "let's meet at the Rose Cafe at 6 p.m."

"Nice try, MJ. We'll meet at Cha Cha Chicken at 5:30."

The Rose Cafe in Venice used to be a great place to eat, but they remodeled and it became very expensive. I knew Big Al wouldn't want to go there because he'd be like a bull in a China shop, but I felt the need to assert myself somehow. I always felt like a child around him, and at times I acted like a rather bratty kid. What the hell was I doing?

He didn't even wait for my acknowledgment as to the time and place but walked away to his car. It felt like he didn't really care if I showed up or not. He'd be there and eat a hearty meal alone if need be.

Since I had about seven to eight hours with nothing to do, I took myself to Venice Beach. I'm not a beach girl, but since it was winter, there weren't many people there and it gave me some quiet time to contemplate.

Otto's revelation left me feeling disturbed and as I walked along the water's edge, dodging the waves that were crashing toward me, I had to admit to myself — it hadn't even occurred to me that Aaron might be the one who murdered all those people. There were five in all. That's a lot of people to kill with a knife. In New Orleans there would have been three of them to one of him. Wouldn't they have overpowered him? Was he that strong?

I knew that rage was a powerful emotion and if his victims were drugged out, their movements would have been slow; they may not have even seen it coming. I really needed to get more information about Luke's New Orleans family.

The more I thought about his family lying slaughtered in his living room way back then, the more the images of my father came to me, unbidden. Mainly, images of blood splattered all over the place. I needed to sit down. The sand was cold and it wasn't a pleasant sensation, but sitting gave me strength and I didn't have to worry about falling if I fainted.

Luke seemed to be doing so well. I couldn't help but wonder if maybe I'm the one who needed to go into some intense therapy about my trauma over finding my father all those years ago. Images of him sitting there in all that blood still haunts me and no matter how much I drink, or how busy I make myself, or how many dysfunctional relationships I get into, those images still haunt me.

***

When I arrived at the colorful Cha Cha Chicken place, Big Al was already there waiting in line. There was actually a line and this indicated to me that the food must be good.

I was starving. I was glad that Big Al had arrived early so we were able to order pretty quickly and find a table to sit in their outdoor seating.

I had heard of Cha Cha Chicken, but had never eaten there. I looked around and saw I was surrounded by bright and happy colors of the Caribbean: yellows, greens, blues, oranges. It was mainly family seating, with some big tables inhabited by bigger groups of people. But there were plenty of smaller tables to accommodate two to three people, so we had our privacy.

"I hope you don't mind, but I also ordered you a couple of beers. I figured, since you're not an alcoholic, you would enjoy a nice cold one with your chicken."

I stared at him in confusion with my mouth most likely hanging open and was about to challenge him, when he laughed and said, "Just kidding, MJ. You know, you need to lighten up."

I could feel my cheeks start to burn. Even though he was kidding, it still felt like an insult to me, or like there was something wrong with me because I took life so seriously. I wanted to tell him that if he had my life, he'd be taking things seriously too. But I stopped myself, since I actually did know about his life. He shared freely in the AA meetings, so I knew all about his violent past and that he had even spent time in prison, not to mention his violent upbringing. I had no winning argument when it came to whose life was worse. He won, hands down.

Our food came remarkably fast and as we started to dig in, he looked me in the eyes and asked, "So, MJ, you didn't take that drink last night. Why not?"

"I'm not sure. Maybe to prove to myself that I wasn't an alcoholic?"

"So why did it occur to you to give me a call if you're not one? Or, why not have the drink? How could that harm you, if you're not an alcoholic?"

"Okay, you got me. I go back and forth about this, Al." Although I called him Al to his face, in my private reference to him, he was always Big Al.

"Maybe it's time for us to start talking about working an AA 12-step program."

I knew that going to the few AA meetings I had attended, bringing the pastries, and talking to Big Al was all leading to this, but I wasn't so sure about it yet.

We had ordered some spicy Cuban fries and when they came, we sat and munched on them for a while before I said, "Look, I don't mind coming to the meetings. I like to listen to other people's stories. Mostly, it makes me feel good about myself because I haven't gotten myself in a boatload of trouble like a lot of alcoholics. This is why I keep wondering if I have a problem, you understand?"

"Okay, fair enough," and after popping a few fries in his mouth and washing it down with his non-alcoholic ginger beer, he continued, "What's really stopping you from committing to this program, MJ?"

Mmmmm, he was asking me a serious question. I assumed it was because I didn't want to admit I was an alcoholic, or that I didn't want to give up alcohol.

I didn't answer and we sat and silently ate our delicious jerk chicken. As I contemplated his question, I wondered why I hadn't eaten at Cha Cha Chicken before.

After a bit, we both gave up on using our utensils and dug in with our fingers. I looked up and saw Big Al's beard full of sauce, along with a big smear on the tip of his nose, and started laughing. I laughed so hard, my stomach ached and all I could do was point at him and hold my stomach.

When he reached out his enormous paw and smeared my nose with sauce, my laughter subdued a bit, but I was still chuckling when I used my napkin to wipe it off.

"See, you do have a sense of humor, MJ."

Yeah I did, and it felt good. I didn't need a glass of wine, or a shot of vodka to enjoy my meal with Big Al.

But it was Big Al. He was special. It wouldn't be like this with anyone else.

Chapter 34

We agreed that I would start reading the Big Book and find a Big Book study meeting to go to. At least I think that's what he called it. It was a meeting where they studied parts of the Alcoholic Anonymous Book. I liked reading and loved anything that had to do with psychology, so I had no trouble agreeing to it.

As a psychologist, I had a bias around addictions that didn't match up with a 12-step program. I took a more psychological view on why people started using and continued to use, whereas, the 12-step programs believed it was a disease, just like if you had diabetes.

I had a lot of trouble with thinking of drinking as a disease. I was raised with my mother berating my father for drinking and not being man enough to just stop, so I developed a strong bias along the lines of addictions being more a matter of being weak and not having enough will power to stop.

As I was driving home from Cha Cha Chicken, I thought about what Big Al asked me. What was the real reason why I didn't want to embrace the AA program? I mean, if I found out I wasn't an Alcoholic, I could always quit and start drinking again. Right? So, what was I afraid of?

Nothing came to mind, so I tucked it into the dark recesses of my mind where I tucked a lot of things I didn't want to face. So like Scarlet O'Hara in "Gone With the Wind", I decided to 'think about it tomorrow'.

***

In the morning, I ate the left over Jerk Chicken from Cha Cha's for breakfast and it tasted just as good as the night before. I could see it was going to become one of my favorite places to eat.

I had to laugh at the thought of Franny going there. With her supermodel clothes, she wouldn't really fit in. But I wasn't being fair to her. She'd never been a stuck up rich kid. She just couldn't help the way she looked, the money she had to buy things, and her beautiful tall, slim body. It was all natural to her and not her fault. I certainly didn't hold it against her, but had a hard time imagining her eating there, especially with her hands.

The clothes I had worn the night before were spotted with sauce and I thought I had been very careful. Of course, we didn't really have to eat with our hands, it was just more fun with Big Al.

As I looked out my windows that overlooked my remodel, I saw the construction crew doing their thing. It was like watching an old black and white movie — a lot of action, but no sound. I knew that when I put my hearing aids in, I would be hearing a lot of noise, so I kept them off and enjoyed a quiet time drinking my morning coffee as I gazed out the windows at the ocean.

I spent the day working on some marketing aspects of my practice until my first client of the day came in late afternoon. I scheduled people later in the day because it helped me stay sober. I had never had a drink before a session and wasn't about to start.

The day passed quickly and after my sessions, the night seemed to stretch out before me and the feeling of loneliness grew inside. I was so tempted to call Jesse but knew that would be the very wrong thing to do, so I contemplated either calling Franny, or going over to visit Aunt Carrie.

In the end, I decided to stay put and watch a funny movie on my iPad, which turned out to not be such a good idea. The characters were all drinking at a fancy lounge and it triggered my urge to have a cocktail in a fancy bar. I hadn't frequented fancy bars since before I met Gideon, so don't know why I got triggered.

I turned my iPad off and, feeling restless, called Big Al.

"Hey."

"I know it's late and I'm sorry if I woke you, but you did tell me to call you any time."

"Yup, that's right. Any time, day or night."

"Even 2 a.m. in the morning?"

"MJ, when are you going to trust that I'm here for you? When are you going to trust that others care about you just as much as you care about everyone else?"

"What do you mean? I have people who care about me. I know that Franny cares about me. I trust her."

"Okay. You may be right, but ask yourself this, when you're in trouble, is she there for you, like you're there for her? Who comes first in your friendship, you or her? If there's a question about which is prioritized, you or her, which one comes first?"

I could feel my defenses rise, "It's a mutual friendship. We both count."

"Uh-huh."

I waited for him to continue, so when he didn't, I just hung up on him. He clearly sparked a nerve. Yes, Franny was there for me in an emergency. She was there to help me out financially if I ever needed it. She helped me the year before when I was dealing with the murder of the anonymous caller, Joe.

But I had to be honest, nine out of ten times, I gave in to her. I was always second fiddle. But I chose that, didn't I? I hated being in the limelight. I was happy to be second to her, to bask in her brightness. She was the star; not I. Big Al had no idea how our friendship worked. He had no business critiquing me about who came first.

I had worked myself to a fevered pitch and went to my little kitchenette to grab my vodka before I realized that it was all gone and I hadn't replaced it. Damn.

Now, who would I call? It was late at night and I wouldn't bother Aunt Carrie, but I could call Franny, right? She'd understand. But then I looked at the time and realized that I couldn't call her so late. She would just ignore my call or not answer. And I was sure she had her phone turned off so she'd get her sleep. But, did that mean she thought of herself first above me, or was she just setting boundaries in order to get a good nights sleep?

I never thought about Franny not being available in the middle of the night for me as her being selfish or putting herself first before me, but after talking to Big Al, I started thinking about it and became more and more irate. I could not stop these negative thoughts about Franny.

It was already 3 a.m. and I had become so angry that I called Big Al again. I didn't give a care if I woke him or not.

He did not answer and the call went immediately to voicemail. So much for his promise that I could trust him to answer any time, day or night.

When his voice mail finished, I said, "How dare you get me all worked up and then not answer me, you liar. See, I can't trust you, can I. You lied to me!"

It was one of those times when I wished we still used landline phones, so I could have slammed the receiver down, showing him my absolute displeasure and feeling of betrayal.

A minute after I punched the disconnect button on my cell, it rang. It was Big Al.

"Hello," I said in a tiny voice.

"I'm here, MJ. I'm here."

Chapter 35

My next meeting with Luke was with him alone. He had continued to get treatment for PTSD at the clinic and continued to see Dr. Holder. He told me that he was not taking the medication she prescribed, and they were going to work with him without it because he felt so good.

He told me that he had gone back to work and his friendship with John was strong. There didn't seem to be any negative backlash toward him from his fellow employees. He told me that most of them knew what happened and seemed sympathetic, so Luke didn't feel awkward.

After getting caught up with all of this, I asked him if he would tell me more about his family from New Orleans. I wanted to know more about his life growing up there and also I wanted to know more about his mother.

"Dr. Lange, I loved my mama. She was a beautiful woman and she had the best singing voice. She used to sing me to sleep every night and she'd hum throughout the days. She had a job singing with one of the jazz bands down there, but the work was at night so my Auntie Bessie came over at night and stayed with me."

"Can you tell me a little bit more about your Aunt Bessie? I'm assuming she was your mother's sister?"

"Auntie Bessie was only nineteen when I was born. She babysat me until I was about eight."

"Did your mother still work at night when you were eight?"

"No, she'd stopped before that, but went out a lot at night. I didn't know why she was gone at night back then, but when I got older, I knew she was out with people, mostly men, using drugs. She changed a lot when I started going to school."

"How so?"

"For one thing, she stopped singing. I hardly ever saw her because she was usually still in bed when I got up and got myself to school. When I did get home in the afternoon she was up, but stumbled around a lot. She had trouble walking."

"How did you manage with all that, being so young?"

"Auntie Bessie would come over. She took care of me. Sometimes she cooked for me or she helped me with my homework."

"So, Luke, how did you feel about your mother being gone so much?"

"Well, Dr. Lange, at first I was scared. I thought something was wrong with her. I thought she was going to die because she kept falling down and slurring her words. I tried to be really quiet and really good, so she wouldn't have to worry about me. When I got older and started to understand that she was using drugs, I just got angry."

I wanted to know where his grandparents were during all of this. He told me they never lived in New Orleans and he had never met them. They had disowned his mother when she moved to New Orleans to pursue a singing career. They thought she was giving up the promise of a nursing career, following in her mother's footsteps.

"After your mother was killed, they never came?"

"Nope, and I didn't know who they were or where they lived."

"What about your Aunt Bessie? How did she get to New Orleans in the first place? Was she also disowned by her parents?"

"I don't really know. She lived down the street from us forever, I think with her boyfriend. I saw him some, but he kept his distance. It was like a secret, so that's just how it was."

I then wondered aloud how his Aunt Bessie happened to be at his house when they were killed.

"Auntie Bessie started using too, I guess when I was in the third grade maybe, when Mama was getting worse. That's why she never babysat me anymore. She and Mama were almost always high. Then Mama started bringing men home and they'd turn on the music and slow dance until they'd drop on the sofa and nod out."

"Where were you when all of this was going on in the house?"

"I stayed away as long as I could. I'd usually stay at a nearby park. When it got dark out, I had to come home. By that time, they were usually gone, so I was able to go to sleep."

"How did you eat? Who bought groceries for you?"

"There was usually things like crackers and peanut butter, bread and milk. I didn't starve. Also, I ate the lunch the school provided and kept the things like apples or bananas — things I could save to eat later. Some of the kids left some of their food on their trays and I was able to grab some of that on occasion to eat later."

Listening to Luke tell his story touched my heart. I felt deeply for this poor kid, alone in the world with virtually no family support. He was basically on his own at a very early age, watching his mother and aunt destroy themselves, being helpless to do anything about it. I wondered where social services had been, but then realized that sometimes being in the system was just as bad.

Thinking about his situation, I also could only imagine what might have happened to his mother, a beautiful black woman singer in New Orleans with no family support, losing her dream as a singer, maybe regretting her choices, losing faith. The way Luke talked about her, she seemed like a loving young mother with a lot of talent who maybe got in over her head and didn't know how to get back. Maybe if she had had the chance to live longer, she would have gotten clean and sober, and Luke and his mother could have revived that earlier connection.

It was the end of our session and I still had a lot of questions for Luke. But it had been an intense session and both Luke and I were spent from stirring up a lot of emotions. Luke had cried a couple of times during our discussion and I realized that he was trying so hard to live a normal life.

He told me that he had called the educational psychologist to get a date for testing, but she couldn't see him for a couple more weeks. We made an appointment for the next week and Luke reached out to me and hugged me before he left.

I returned his hug, but he hung on far longer than an end-of-session hug, so I gently pulled away and looked at him with a question, without speaking.

"Dr. Lange, you remind me of my mama before she went bad. She was so kind and I still miss her, even though she's been dead for a long time."

At that moment, I wasn't so sure I wanted to remind him of his mother. She was murdered, and no one knew who did it.

Chapter 36

The day after my session with Luke, Dr. Holden reached out to me to discuss his progress. I told her that Luke seemed so happy most of the time, which wasn't what I expected at all, but that I thought our session the day before had started to open him up to his childhood trauma.

"I started asking him about his family in New Orleans. It was the first time Luke showed any kind emotion since the murders of his roommates."

"I see."

"Dr. Holden, what do you make of him seemingly so okay with those murders? I would have expected to see a bigger reaction. His moving back into the house doesn't compute with this kind of trauma. Usually there is more avoidance of things around it, not plunging right back into a life as if nothing happened."

"I know. It bothers me too, MJ. The clinic also doesn't really know how to treat him either since he's not showing any real distress. I'm thinking of pausing the PTSD treatment and waiting to see what comes up for him."

"Would you still see him?"

"Of course, but I think he's bonded the most with you, so I'd want you to keep seeing him weekly and I'll see him every other week for a while until something comes to a head. Or not.

"Why don't you continue to question him about his family in New Orleans. He's never had any real therapy or treatment for that trauma. He may have some kind of dissociation or long term shock going on. I think it best to ferret out what happened after they were murdered."

"I agree. The details seem hazy. His brother, Aaron, was there in New Orleans and from what I could gather, he swept Luke up and brought him out here to California. And I have no idea how that all happened. I think I'm going to have another try with Aaron."

After we hung up, I wasn't sure if I should see Aaron with Luke, or alone. I did have Luke's consent forms saying that I could talk to his doctor and other therapists. And he had signed the authorization for me to talk to family members like, Aaron and Otto.

Since Luke wasn't scheduled to see me for another week, I was eager to move forward. I informed Luke of my intention to see Aaron, then called him and set up an appointment for him to come in alone.

***

Aaron looked a little less like a cowboy when he stepped into my office the next day. He wore faded blue jeans and a t-Shirt, but instead of cowboy boots, he had on sneakers. And no cowboy hat this time.

"Thank you for coming, Aaron," I said as I indicated a seat across from my therapist chair.

"No problem, Dr. Lange, happy to do it. Luke deserves the best."

"Have you gotten together with Luke since the last time you were here?"

I knew he hadn't because Luke told me that he didn't want anything to do with "those people".

Aaron looked over at me with a slight bend to his head and shrugged.

"I guess not."

He threw his hands up and sighed.

"Why do you think he doesn't want to have anything to do with you and your father?"

"Probably because we were being assholes when he first came to live with us. Not that we've changed, but it was a particularly bad time between my father and me when he first came."

"Why was that?"

"My father hadn't wanted me to go meet Luke in the first place. He told me that Luke didn't belong with us. He said too much time had passed and it was no longer a good idea for him to try to be part of the family. I asked him whose fault that was, but he just ignored me as usual."

I asked Aaron what he remembered after Luke found his family murdered.

Aaron explained that Luke wouldn't talk to him. Luke had been admitted to the hospital for shock and was kept for observations for a few days. Luke didn't say much and hardly knew Aaron was there. It was the first time the half-brothers had met. Aaron had been excited to meet Luke, but after the murders, the reunion took a different turn.

I imagined that Luke associated Aaron with the deaths of his family, so probably wasn't so thrilled to meet him. They were strangers and Luke hadn't even known he had a brother. There was a lot for the then teenager, Luke Brown, to deal with after the murders.

"Luke didn't want to leave New Orleans because he wanted to stay and help find who murdered his family, but I persuaded him to come back to California to get away from it all for a while; that the police could contact him by phone if they needed anything else from him."

After a long pause, he continued, "I don't know. Maybe it was a bad idea to bring him out here. It didn't seem to help much and all the hope and expectations I had about finding my long lost brother kind of fizzled out when he mainly kept to himself and didn't want to engage with me.

"Dr. Lange, I have tried to make him part of my family; I really have. But he doesn't want anything to do with me, or us. I've mostly kept my distance after trying so many times to befriend him. There's only so much one can do."

"Aaron, did Luke ever tell you he might know who killed his family? Did he tell you he saw anything, or knew of possible enemies?"

"Nope. And I didn't ask. If you had seen him those months after, you wouldn't have asked him either. He was like a zombie. All I could think about was getting him back to California where he didn't have to be in that awful place."

As I continued to question Aaron, it didn't seem to lend any insights or give me anything that would have been useful in finding out what the family secrets were. I ended the session and he agreed to be available if we needed to talk again.

Chapter 37

Talking to Aaron didn't seem to give me any added knowledge about what went down in New Orleans either. It seemed most likely it was a drug deal gone bad. My heart went out to Luke though. He had been so young at the time he lost his family in such a brutal manner, and being the one to have found them was a major trauma.

I wasn't sure what my next steps were. I knew I wasn't going to solve the crimes, although I had a gut instinct that if they were solved, the mystery of Luke would be unleashed. However, I had no idea why my thoughts were going in that direction.

I intuitively knew that I needed to solve the mystery of Luke and his half-brother and father, so that was the direction I was going to take. I felt that the murder mysteries and the family mysteries were somehow entwined, but for the life of me, I logically couldn't see how they might be connected.

There was such an uneasy feeling I got around this family. The murders in New Orleans were never solved and it was beginning to look like the murders of Luke's roommates were also not going to get solved. This seemed more than a mere coincidence to me. There had to be some kind of connection. Why didn't the police see it? Or, if they did, no one was telling me about it.

I dialed Detective Nordell and left him a message asking him to call me if there was any new information he could tell me about the murders in Los Angeles. Surely they would have found something. It seemed to me they'd be doing background checks on Luke's roommate; talking to their parents, the neighbors, and especially taking a look into who might have been selling them their drugs.

Waiting for the detective to call me back, I took one of my legal pads and started taking down notes. When I write things down, sometimes vital information gets revealed to me; I get new ideas about what's going on. I do this with my clients all the time. When their symptoms don't match what they are telling me, I need a way to flesh out what's really going on in their current lives, as well as the past.

I could tell story after story of clients withholding vital information that was needed in order for them to heal. Usually, they weren't withholding on purpose, but the information either seemed unimportant to them, or they just didn't remember.

Now, I sat on my sofa with my legal pad on my lap and started writing about Luke, hoping that my unconscious would spit out something of importance. I understood that we were constantly taking in all kinds of cues and information that we aren't always conscious of, so I was hoping the writing would put all the pieces together and give me an answer to some of my questions.

As I wrote, I noted that Luke was an only child of a young woman with few resources and abandoned by his biological father. He grew up in a partly sketchy neighborhood in New Orleans, but did go to school and was looked after by his aunt until he was around eight years old.

He didn't do very well in school, but there didn't seem to be anyone in his family, or in the school system that looked into his poor performance. Like a lot of schools, they just passed him on until he got to high school where his large size and physical ability was noticed by the football coach and he was given some academic help in order for him to play for the team. Playing football was where he was finally able to shine, but his family ignored it and he had no support, leaving him feeling alone, angry, and hurt.

His mother, aunt, and mother's boyfriend were all drug users and Luke was basically left to take care of himself after the age of eight. His way out was going to be a football scholarship, but when his family was murdered, that seemed to have disappeared. Or Luke, himself, rejected the scholarship due to his decision to never play football again after the two-fold drama of his family failing to come to his last game, and then his discovery of the murders.

I stopped writing at this point because up until the murders of his family, the details seemed pretty clear. Where it started to get muddy was when Aaron showed up immediately after the murders. I wondered if this really was a coincidence, or did Aaron have something to do with it? Luke and Aaron didn't seem to be able to talk in detail about how Luke got to California, and it seemed vague to me.

Did Aaron coerce Luke into coming back to California with him from New Orleans? Did the authorities suggest it? Otto had said he hadn't wanted Luke to come, but maybe that was just Aaron's impression. When I spoke with Otto alone, he seemed to feel guilty and I got the impression he was all for helping Luke out.

Once Luke lived with Aaron and Otto, he couldn't get out of that place fast enough. I know he said they were arguing about him a lot and he felt responsible, but I kept thinking there was something more. A family secret no one is talking about? Or, maybe I was just frustrated because I couldn't get a clear picture of the dynamics of the family and needed more information. Maybe I just needed more time for it to make sense.

I've seen clients for up to two years before they feel safe enough to tell me some horrendous secret they had hidden from everyone. Once the cat is out of the bag, everything makes sense, but I can't hurry the reveal. It has to come in its own time and I had to remind myself of that.

If Luke were to keep living what he considered his normal life, and his father and brother left him alone, I may never find out their family secrets. Luke could decide to stop coming for therapy and he would no longer be my client.

But I couldn't let any of this go. I had to keep digging. I was sure there was some connection between the murders and Luke's family.

What I kept coming back to was the fact that Otto called me with concerns about Aaron. Was it a coincidence that Aaron was in both cities when the murders took place? Was there a motivation for him to have killed Luke's family and then Luke's roommates? Did Luke somehow think that Aaron was responsible for these murders, but didn't have the evidence, so he kept away from Aaron?

Or, were both of these really drug deals gone bad? Were the bad guys responsible and very clever at not leaving any evidence behind? It just seemed like too much of a coincidence to me.

***

Just as I was putting my pen and pad away, my phone buzzed and I saw it was Detective Nordell.

"Hi, Detective Nordell. Thanks for calling me back so promptly."

"Dr. Lange, I'm sorry to say that I have nothing new to report. The people who were at the party at Luke's house all check out with alibis. They were all either college students going to Santa Monica College, or young friends of the roommates. They all agreed that the party petered out around one a.m. and most of them had left by two."

"I see."

"However," he went on, "no one is admitting to how they got the drugs. They all admitted that they'd been at a few parties at that location before and just assumed it was the roommates who got them. They told me they had brought beer, cheap wine, and snacks like chips and salsa. They were asked to contribute some cash for the drugs if they used them. It actually seemed quite organized for a college party. So we don't know who might have had an issue around the drugs. It could be that one or both of the roommates were the only ones who had the connection to a dealer, so we may never find out who sold to them, or even if the murders had anything to do with a dealer."

"So you haven't collected any useful evidence at all?"

"I'm sorry to tell you that we have not. But there is a little good news."

"I'm all ears."

"We are familiar with all the petty drug dealers in the area who sell small amounts of cocaine, crystal meth, MDMA, those sort of party drugs. The roommates' use was small-time stuff, so we doubt there was any big drug deal gone bad. These petty dealers are not usually violent and mostly sell in order to maintain their own habits."

"I don't understand. If you know who they are, why don't you arrest them?"

"These guys come and go, Dr. Lange. They only sell to their young friends, and only from referrals. We don't have the manpower to spend on these petty dealers. There are bigger fish to catch. We were able to bring in the petty dealers who are still in business, but we couldn't get any confessions or information out of any of them. All the fingerprints and other forensic evidence we recovered was what we'd expect to find around a party of that sort."

"What's the good news?" I wasn't hearing anything positive with this information and thought I might have missed it.

"We can rule out a drug deal gone bad, or that the murders had anything to do with the party-goers."

"So, that leaves who for suspects?"

"That's the bad news; we don't have any suspects. We can't find anything that the girls may have been involved in to give us a break."

This *was* bad news. I wondered if I should tell him that Aaron was in both New Orleans and Santa Monica during both of the murders.

I couldn't think of any reason not to tell him and I wouldn't be breaking anyone's confidentiality. Otto and Aaron were not my clients and I had no contract with them, nor did I tell them that anything said between us was confidential.

This is where I sometimes get sticky with the law and ethics of my profession. I should have called my association and gotten clarity about confidentiality before I talked to Otto and Aaron.

Since I had Detective Nordell on the phone, I made a quick decision about how to let him know Aaron was in both cities at the time of the murders.

"Detective Nordell, have you looked into Aaron Haas?"

"Yes, we have. We looked into both Aaron and his father."

"What did you find, if anything?"

"We know Otto was up north with his orange orchards, and that Aaron was actually down here in Los Angeles."

"I see. So you have no proof Aaron could have been involved in the murders here in Los Angeles?"

"Ms. Lange, why are you asking this? Do you have information that we should be looking into?"

"No, I don't. It's just that Aaron was in both New Orleans and Los Angeles during each of the murders, but I guess you already know that."

He confirmed that they were aware of Aaron's whereabouts in both cases and did say that they haven't totally ruled Aaron out, but there was no evidence and no motivation for Aaron to have killed both the family and roommates.

I tried not to sound disappointed. I was hoping that maybe Aaron would be a good lead for the Detective, but they seemed to already be on top of it. We hung up and I went into my kitchen to scrounge up something with sugar in it.

If I couldn't drink, then I was going to eat sugar.

I found chocolate covered almonds and sat down with them as I looked over the construction site of my new home.

Secretly, I was glad that Aaron wasn't a suspect. When he wasn't arguing with his father, I rather liked him. He seemed to genuinely feel bad about Luke and his situation and had wanted to be of help to him.

As I ate my chocolates, I reminded myself that it wasn't my job to solve the murders. But it was my job to solve the family dynamics in the Haas house. I knew there was something negative going on between that household and Luke. I just didn't know what it could be, and wondered what it was that I was missing.

Chapter 38

I needed a break. My brain was working overtime and I felt a migraine coming on, so I got up and made myself a strong cup of coffee. The caffeine often kept the migraine away, or at least made the pain less.

Sipping my black coffee, I continued to try and figure out what my next step would be with Luke. But the migraine came on with a vengeance.

I still hadn't gotten drapes or shutters for my office apartment and the sun streaming in made my eyes hurt so I opened my sofa bed and laid down covering my face with a blanket.

I knew that if I could just go to sleep for a couple of hours, the migraine might be gone when I woke up. I prayed this would be the case.

***

When I woke, it was dusk and I saw that the construction crew had already left.

My migraine was gone and I breathed a sigh of relief, but as I fully awakened, I had some memory or thought that was tickling my consciousness and I knitted my brows in concentration to try and figure out what it was.

Nothing concrete came to mind, but there was a fleeting shadow of a memory, or an image, or a thought that was just beyond my reach. I sat up and put my head in my hands as I rocked myself back and forth in a soothing rhythm, hoping that it would allow my subconscious to reveal what it was hiding.

I had had nothing of substance to eat except the chocolate covered almonds and I realized I was famished. I went to see if I had anything I could eat in my refrigerator, but quickly changed my mind and called Franny to see if she'd like to go with me to the new restaurant I had learned about, the Cha Cha Chicken.

I was craving the jerk chicken and thought it would be fun to see if Franny was still game to eat in such a casual and relaxed atmosphere. At college, we used to slum it all the time, but as Franny matured, she tended to dress for dinner and leaned toward the more upscale, expensive places.

She agreed to go, and I told her to wear old clothing she never wanted to wear again. This sparked her interest and we agreed to meet there since it was located between us. I had an ulterior motive in inviting Franny out to eat. She was a good listener at times and could pick up on things I couldn't necessarily figure out. Of course, her interpretation was often the opposite of mine, but it was like her playing the Devil's advocate and I often got inspiration from it.

We met outside of Cha Cha's and I saw that Franny had her dark hair up in a high pony tail. Her tall, athletic body was adorned with a cuddly sweatshirt and an old pair of Levi's. Her feet were stuck in an ugly pair of old Ugg boots.

She had taken me seriously and dressed down, but even when she dresses down, she still looks fabulous. Like I said, she can't help it.

Since I had been there once and the food Big Al had ordered for us was delicious, I suggested the same thing. She ordered a beer and I had water with lemon.

Looking around at the bold colors, she said, "How did you find this place? I love it. I just hope the food is as good as the atmosphere."

Franny is not a snob. She delights in almost everything. She's one of the most positive people I know — unless she's dealing with family and her wealth. She has to go to meetings with her financial advisors and others regarding her finances and she really hates it. I, on the other hand, have no money so don't have a clue what she has to go through. Most of us think having money makes life easier, but I've seen the stress it causes my good friend and wouldn't wish that on anyone.

After we licked the last traces of jerk chicken from our fingers, Franny asked me how things were going.

When I started to tell her about the stalemate around the murder of Luke's roommates, Franny was all ears. She loves gossip, although she rarely indulged in it herself. She's very good at keeping secrets; maybe too good. This is nice for me because I feel I can tell her anything and I know she won't ever disclose any information that I give her. Does this border on ethical misconduct on my part when it pertains to clients? Maybe; but I trust her more than I trust another colleague, or even my own therapist.

"Don't tell me you're trying to figure out the murder, MJ."

"No, I'm not," I lied, "but it does seem like there is an awful lot of similarity between the two, don't you think?"

"I suppose you're right, but it's been eighteen years between them. Why would a murderer wait eighteen years between a killing spree? And who would be that connected to Luke that they'd do the same kind of murder around him eighteen years later? I mean, he's no longer in New Orleans, so anyone there wouldn't be here, right? Seems to me, the murders don't have anything to do with each other and it's a mere coincidence that the second murder here in Los Angeles happened to be in Luke's place. Seems more logical to me that these were both drug related incidents, don't you think?"

"Wait, say that again."

"That it's more logical to think of these murders as separate entities, related more to drug deals going bad?"

"No, what you said before. Something about him no longer living in New Orleans, so there wouldn't be a connection."

"Okay. Just that he's living in Los Angeles now, so it doesn't seem like anyone from New Orleans would come all the way to Los Angeles in order to do another killing in his house."

There it was. The piece of the puzzle I felt was missing. That's it! Whoever murdered Luke's family in New Orleans wasn't from there. It had to be someone from California and there were only two possibilities, Aaron or Otto.

Why didn't the police see this as clearly as I was seeing it now that Franny pointed it out?

"I had a migraine today and when I woke up, it was gone, but I had an impression of something that I had missed around these murders."

"What was it?"

"I didn't know until you mentioned the idea that no one from New Orleans would be killing someone in Los Angeles eighteen years later. Luke hadn't had any friends or family in New Orleans, so there wouldn't be anyone there with a vendetta against him. He was only a teenager at the time of the murders in New Orleans and wasn't able to come up with any suspect for the police, so why would a drug dealer come hunting for a kid in California, especially eighteen years later? And, if it did involve Luke knowing something, why wasn't Luke the target instead of his roommates?"

"MJ, what are you saying exactly? Are you implying that his brother did this?"

"It has to do with Luke's family; his father and half-brother. There's just something that feels off with them. I mean, it seems too coincidental that Aaron just happened to be in New Orleans the same time Luke's mother was murdered. Then, he just happened to be in Los Angeles the same time Luke's roommates were murdered."

"MJ, there are coincidences in the world. Just because he was in town both times of the murder doesn't mean there is cause and effect. It just means he was in town when both murders happened. Besides, you told me you weren't trying to solve the murders, you were trying to figure out what the deal was involving his father and brother, right? Why not stay with that? Seems like you may get more accomplished focusing on that. Let the police figure out who murdered all of them. It's really none of your business. I mean, unless the murderer is Luke, then you might be in jeopardy, right?"

"You said Luke. Why would you include him?"

The minute she suggested that Luke might be the murderer, I felt that inner panic and fear. Ever since I hadn't realized that Mike Rimichi was posing as a detective, I had lost my confidence and no longer trusted my instincts. Did I know for sure that Luke wasn't responsible? I mean, logic would dictate he'd be the primary suspect. He certainly had the time and means to kill his New Orleans family, but the police were pretty sure he wouldn't have had the time to kill his roommates.

However, in both situations, Luke had been betrayed. Was his hurt, anger, and betrayal big enough for him to do such a horrific act? I just couldn't see Luke doing that.

Unless. . .

"I don't know Luke like you do. You've seen him longer than I did, so I'd go with your impression. But, think about it. If these weren't drug-related murders, who else would have had the biggest motivation?"

When Franny interrupted my thoughts, I looked at her with both annoyance and interest. She was seeing this through fresh eyes. I had become attached to Luke and felt sorry for him, a bad combination. I was even getting attached to both Otto and Aaron.

But good people do bad things all the time. There was surely something bad going on in their household. Could it maybe that it was the murders they were hiding? Was Otto protecting Aaron, but feeling guilty? Is that why he brought up the possibility of Aaron as a suspect? Was Aaron protecting Otto? Highly unlikely, in my opinion. Or, was the tension I was feeling between them brought on by one of them knowing or suspecting the other was the murderer?

Or, was there another sinister person behind the scenes who needed the murders to take place? Did they need Aaron gone and they were setting him up, or maybe even setting Luke up?

That was a new thought. It could be a factor as to motivation. However, if someone was trying to set one or the other of them up, they weren't very good at it. The police weren't finding any clues that would point to any specific person.

Chapter 39

When I got home after dining with Franny, I took the chance that Aaron would be available and called him.

He answered on the first ring. "Dr. Lange, I was just thinking about you."

"Oh, and why is that?"

"I was thinking that maybe I should come again to one of Luke's sessions."

"That's interesting. What do you think that would accomplish?"

"He won't see me. I just want to talk to him. See him in person."

"Maybe it's time you went back home. I'm wondering what your wife is thinking about you staying here in Los Angeles so long. Is she okay with this?"

I hadn't meant to get off on a tangent when I had a specific purpose in calling him, but it did seem strange that he could just stay for weeks at a time in Los Angeles, away from his wife and family. Also, I wondered who was doing Aaron's part in the orchards.

"My wife is a very independent person and she understands why I'm so hung up on helping my bother."

"Aaron, why don't you help me understand, because I really don't get it."

What I really wanted to know was what he was hiding. I wasn't sure how much information I was going to share with him about my concerns around his family, so I asked questions instead. I really wanted to know the details of what had happened after the murders in New Orleans, but it seemed like he was open to talking about his family here in California.

He started out reiterating the fact that he felt his father was the cause of his mother's MS. When I reminded him that he had already told me that, he went on to explain that he felt trapped within the family's orange grove business, especially when he was younger and had first gone to New Orleans to find Luke. He knew he both wanted to be a part of it, and also wanted to break out from under his father's control and forge a life of his own. He just didn't know exactly what life he wanted. His wife understood that and encouraged him to find his own path.

When he learned that he had a half-brother, he was furious that his father hadn't brought Luke into the business. He had suffered all the expectations from his father alone. If he had had a brother to share in some of that, he felt it would have been easier for him.

"So you thought that bringing Luke home would get your father off your back? Maybe Luke would want to take over the business?"

"That was part of it, and still is, but Luke doesn't want anything to do with the business. I don't get it. It's already a successful business; all he'd have to do is come in and learn it. Eventually, he could run it himself if he wanted to. Why would he want to work for pennies at a warehouse?"

"Isn't that what you want to do? Be your own man? Maybe that's what Luke is doing. Being his own person."

"I never thought about it that way. I just assumed he'd want in for the money."

"Is it the money that keeps you there?"

"I'll admit that the money is partly it. But it's also my mom. She needs me. I can't leave her and she won't leave him and come with me, so I'm stuck, doing what Otto needs me to do."

"You have a lot of resentment toward your father."

"You got that right."

I wondered if his resentment was so strong that if properly triggered, he could lose control and slaughter another human being, like he almost did with the orange grove worker.

"Aaron, tell me more about New Orleans. What happened? How did you get Luke to come to California? After the murders, why did you want him to come with you so badly?"

He told me that Luke was so out of it that it wasn't hard to get airline tickets and put him on the plane. Luke resisted, of course, but not by much. The hospital staff who took care of Luke when he was in shock suggested he go with Aaron since Luke didn't have any close friends or family around. He was only seventeen at the time.

Aaron confessed that he still hoped Luke would get assimilated into the family and be the son who took over the business. He admitted that it sounded selfish, but back then he really wanted to get away from his family and the business. He wasn't married yet, nor did he have a family. Being tied down to the orange grove business felt stifling.

He also admitted that once Luke was living with them, he saw how fragile Luke was and didn't know how to help him, so kind of ignored him, hoping his father would be able to do something. He also informed me that

Luke didn't seem to have much common sense, which reminded me that Luke was getting tested and I wanted to follow up on that.

Aaron went on to tell me that things were really bad between him and Otto at that time, so Aaron spent a lot of his time resenting Otto and, in his words, "I was being a prick." He knew Luke had been uncomfortable, but he'd left Luke to his own devices. He was sorry that he hadn't spent more time getting to know Luke like he had originally wanted to do. He realized that most of his motivation around Luke was for Otto to focus on Luke and leave him alone.

"Dr. Lange, it was a crazy time for me. If I had it to do all over again, I would have done it very differently. I'm not sure I would have brought Luke out here to California, but at the time, it seemed like a good idea."

"What happened to Luke's scholarship?"

"I have no idea.There was so much going on with the murders, and then getting the bodies taken care of that it probably just got lost in the wash. I didn't even know there was a scholarship or even that Luke played football. I had never before had to deal with taking care of things after someone died and I felt out of my element. I just wanted to get back to California and not have to deal with any of it.

"Otto actually dealt with the funeral arrangements and burials from California. I thought he should have flown out to New Orleans to help us out, but as usual, he took the easy way out. He just threw money at it and had it taken care of from afar. I had honestly tried to take care of it all, but in the end, Otto did it."

A more accurate picture was emerging of the family dynamics. Otto was a man used to being in control of everything, including his emotions. He wasn't used to sharing inner struggles and Aaron needed a father who paid attention to him and his real needs, not just as a son to carry on the family business. Luke wasn't even in the picture until the murders.

Having Luke added to an already dysfunctional family would add more pressure to an already stressed household. I wondered how Aaron's mother had reacted to all of this.

"Once Luke came home with you, how did your mother take it?"

He sounded surprised, "It was her idea for me to go to New Orleans to bring him back in the first place."

"You mean, after the murders?"

"No, before the murders. She knew about Luke all along and had wanted Otto to do the right thing by him. I'd heard them arguing over this since I was a kid, but never really understood that the person they were arguing about was actually my brother. It was only the week before I went to New Orleans to meet him that I finally grasped it."

This was news to me. I realized that Luke was the family secret. Otto and his wife Isabelle knew about him, but they had kept him a secret from everyone else, including Aaron. I can still remember an old mentor of mine saying, "Secrets make you crazy."

I was curious about Isabelle and thought it possible that she may be another missing link I hadn't known about. What role did she play in all of this? Surely she wouldn't be the murderer because of her MS, but after all, as Franny reminded me, my job is not to find the murderer, but to unravel the family dysfunction.

Chapter 40

After my call with Aaron, my mind wouldn't stop. I was nowhere near unraveling this family dysfunction. I couldn't understand why they were so weirdly secretive about everything.

It seemed pretty straightforward that Otto and his wife didn't have the best relationship, but that Otto had tried to just suck it up and do the right thing. Except his wife wasn't happy. She had been betrayed by him, but for some reason wanted his illegitimate child to come and live with them.

What was her story, anyway? She was a privileged woman, but unhappy with her marriage. Whatever stressors she had most likely caused stress in her body as she succumbed to her medical condition. It seems like she could have left at any time, especially in the early days when Otto left her and journeyed to New Orleans, fathering another son and then abandoning the child.

I wondered if there was any way I could interview Otto's wife, or maybe Aaron's wife. I was just getting the male side of the story and thought perhaps the females in the family would be able to shed more light on the family dynamics.

After getting permission from Luke to talk to Isabelle and Sarah, Aaron's wife, I got their numbers from Aaron. Although he was reluctant to have me speak to either one of them, but finally agreed and texted me their numbers. He reminded me that his mother, Isabelle, had a difficult time with speech, so wasn't sure she'd be much help. He told me that her caregiver would be able to help interpret for her as best she could.

I wasn't sure what I was going to ask them, but maybe just some general background of why the men were all so alienated and either angry at each other, or withholding.

***

It was a long and arduous phone call with Isabelle and I felt guilty for putting her through the questions and concerns. She was not in good shape and her caregiver finally stopped the interview, telling me that Isabelle was getting really tired and showing a lot of frustration because she couldn't make herself understood like she wanted.

Maybe it was too late for Isabelle to offer what she knew. I thought that Sarah would probably have more to say about the past, even if it was only gossip. But surely she would have knowledge about Aaron.

Sarah was happy to talk to me on the phone. Her voice was light and airy and sounded almost like a child's.

She reiterated some of the things that Aaron had told me, but then she said, "Look, I know you're trying to help Luke, but Luke doesn't want help. He has shunned all of us for a long time. He didn't even want to meet his nephew after Jake was born. It hurt my feelings, and I think Aaron really took it to heart."

"What do you mean?"

"Aaron has never stopped trying to connect with Luke. I think he feels guilty about not being able to make things right with Luke. I don't understand it fully, but there's something there between them that I don't understand."

"Sarah, if you were to just guess, what do you think it might be?"

"It's like Aaron is trying to protect Luke, which sounds really weird since Luke is taller and more physically capable than Aaron, but it's like Luke is the child and Aaron's the adult. But Luke doesn't want anything to do with Aaron and Aaron can't seem to let it go."

I let her know that I was listening.

"It's put a wedge between us, this thing with Luke. I've left a couple of times because of it, but came back. I love Aaron, but he's conflicted about Luke and I think he needs help to figure it out. He shuts me down whenever I bring Luke up. It's like it's verboten to talk about him. I've tried to leave it be. I have to if I want to stay married to Aaron, right? I mean, what can I do when he freezes me out like that?"

I had to agree with her that there wasn't much to do if she wanted to stay married to the man. But his constant trying with Luke, despite Luke's rejection of him, didn't make any sense.

After talking to Sarah, it felt more and more like there was something between the brothers that wasn't being shared. Something either happened between them, or there was a spontaneous dislike for each other at their first meeting in New Orleans. Luke was in shock and Aaron was out of his element, still a very young man who had no idea how to cope with certain responsibilities, like what to do with murdered bodies.

The more I thought about it, the more I got to wondering what it was that really happened in New Orleans. Something must have happened between the brothers. Something more than just the shock of the murders for Luke, and Aaron being in over his head. I had no idea what it could be.

Chapter 41

After checking in with Aunt Carrie and Joey, I found myself taking a solitary walk along Main Street in Venice. There weren't a lot of people out and about since the weather had turned chilly, but the stores were open, getting ready for the Christmas sales, even though it wasn't even Thanksgiving yet.

I did a little window shopping and saw some interesting items I thought Franny might like. Since she could buy herself anything she wanted, it was more like trying to find some interesting stones, or art by local artists that would be to her liking.

As I passed a bar, I saw what seemed like happy people sitting inside sipping on hot toddies or Irish coffees and I felt that feeling of loneliness inside of me. I ached to also be sitting inside that bar with someone special.

With those feelings pressing, it was probably the time I should have been looking for an AA meeting. Instead, I kept walking until I made a complete tour up and down Main Street, and then headed home.

I couldn't get Luke and his family out of my head. It just wasn't making any sense and I had to admit, the whole thing felt kind of creepy to me. I mean, Luke's dazzling, cheery smile was so incongruent with what he had experienced with two multiple murders in his homes. Then there was Aaron's desire to keep close to Luke and Otto's rather cold detachment to the entire thing; both seemed odd to me.

The two women didn't seem to be able to shed much light on any of it. Was it just that these men were incapable of showing any kind of real emotions, and kept stuffing their feelings down to where there wasn't any ability to connect with each other?

Maybe they wanted to connect, but didn't know how, which would be typical of the male animal, or at least my experience of many of my male clients.

When I reached my office apartment, it was dark out and I hadn't left the light on, so took my phone out and turned on the flashlight to light my way. I wasn't really scared but the darkness was making me a little nervous.

I had forgotten my appointment with my trauma therapist that week and as the shadows seemed to be jumping about as I moved toward my steps, I realized that I really mustn't miss those sessions. I was getting better, but this kind of thing was a trigger for me and I cursed myself for not leaving the lights on.

Looking over and seeing Aunt Carrie's backyard lit up gave me some sense of safety and I almost ran over to her house to see if April might be home to walk with me up my stairs until I could get my lights on. But then I felt silly because there was probably no body there in the shadows.

I was sure the jumping shadows were just my imagination until I saw a dark figure looming up out of the stairwell.

Instead of screaming or running, I froze. I stood with the light of my phone pointed at the figure and without even breathing, I waited, unable to move, until it came into view.

"Luke," I said, "you scared the bejeebies out of me, what are you doing here?"

"I'm sorry, Dr. Lange. I didn't know what to do. I tried calling you, but it kept going to voicemail, so I just came over."

I looked at my phone and realized that I had several missed calls and texts.

"I'm so sorry, Luke. My phone was turned off, but I usually feel the vibrations. I must have been preoccupied and didn't notice. Here, come up to my office with me."

After I got the lights turned on and we were both settled in our respected chairs, I asked, "What's wrong?"

He looked ashen and startled, like I'd imagine one would look like if they'd seen a ghost.

"I don't know, Dr. Lange, but I don't feel so good."

"Like physically? Have you seen a doctor?"

"No, I'm not sick. I just feel weird."

"Weird?"

"Yeah. Like my head isn't connected to my body. Kind of like I'm floating up above myself. It feels scary. I'm not sure how to describe it."

"Okay, okay. Let's just take some deep breaths together, okay?"

I showed him how to put one of his hands on his abdomen and the other on his chest and then to deep breathe. I did this together with him for a while until the color came back to his face and his shoulders relaxed and he seemed more present. I had assumed he may be having an anxiety or panic attack.

"Okay, Luke, how was that? Are you feeling a little better?"

"Yes I am, Dr. Lange."

"Good, good. Why don't you tell me what's going on. Did something happen?"

"I'm not sure."

"You mean you don't remember, or you don't know if what happened caused this reaction?"

"Aaron called me and wanted to come over. I told him no."

I thought maybe Aaron had come anyway, but Luke said he had not. But since he was scared Aaron *would* come, he locked his doors and hid in his bedroom closet.

"You hid in the closet?"

"Yeah, in my bedroom."

"Can you tell me why you hid in your bedroom closet?"

"I got scared."

"Of Aaron?"

"I don't know. I just got scared after telling Aaron he couldn't come over."

"Okay."

I had a feeling that all of this was leading to something very important and I didn't want to spook him, so I proceeded with caution.

"Do you know why you might be scared of Aaron?"

"Not really."

"Has Aaron ever hurt you, Luke?"

"No. No, Aaron's never hurt me. He's always tried to be nice to me."

"But you're scared of him, right?"

"I think so."

At this point he looked around my office, eyes wide, like he didn't recognize where he was.

"Luke, do you know where you are?"

"I'm here with you."

"Yes, you're here with me, your therapist. We're in my office. Do you remember coming to see me here tonight?"

"I know I was trying to call you when I was in the closet hiding. You didn't answer and I got very scared, so I ran out of my house and came over here to you."

"Okay, Luke, that's good. You came to be with someone you'd feel safe with. That's good. You are safe here. Should we call Dr. Holden?"

When he heard the name of his psychiatrist, he let out a long exhale and said, "I don't want to bother her unless we have to."

I could see that Luke was feeling better and coming back to his more normal self, so I asked him if he would be able to talk more about what made him so scared."

He just looked at me and smiled his dazzling smile, shrugged his shoulders, and said, "Whew, I don't know, Dr. Lange. It was like I was on some weird trip and didn't know exactly what was happening. I felt confused and didn't know which way was up and which way was down. Colors and shapes of things were all distorted and it felt very scary. All I knew to do was to hide. But then it felt like there *was* no place to hide, so then I knew I needed to come and see you."

Chapter 42

I made us both a cup of soothing lavender tea and as we sipped on the tea together, I casually told him that I'd like to call Dr. Holden and get her opinion of what might have happened to him.

I wasn't sure, but thought that he may have slipped into a temporary psychosis brought on by a trigger of some sort from talking to Aaron. I also thought that his symptoms could have been a reaction about the murders that he had been repressing. Maybe Aaron said something to him that opened him up to the painful memories and the horror of what he had seen. It's possible he dissociated in order to handle the trauma. Often past trauma can lead to a person feeling detached from themselves and have no memory of what happened; having a feeling of not being their normal self. I wasn't sure and wanted Dr. Holden to evaluate him.

When she finally called me back, they talked on the phone a bit until Luke handed the phone back to me and

Dr. Holden told me that he seemed to be stable at the moment and that he should try to go stay with his friend John for the night and then come and see her in the morning.

Luke was amenable to doing that and after he left, I sat in my therapist chair and just stared out into space. It was a disquieting experience. I haven't witnessed many psychotic breaks, but I know that the unreality of what the client is experiencing is so very real to them, and it makes the observer also feel unsettled.

I made up my sofa bed and grabbed my pillow, hugging it to my chest as I tried to go to sleep, leaving all the lights on.

This whole thing with Luke was getting to me and I felt like it was way above my ability.

I didn't sleep all night and in the morning called Dr. Holden to ask if I could have a consultation with her, thinking I'd tell her that I needed to transfer him away from my care. It was too scary for me and had triggered a PTSD reaction for me also.

Seeing Luke lose it like he did the night before made me realize that I was vulnerable around him. He was a big guy and if there was something seriously wrong with him, I'd be in a lot of trouble because there was no way I would be able to defend myself against him.

I saw a part of him I had never seen before. He was terrified and was seeing distortions. What if he started seeing a distortion in me and thought I was an enemy? What the hell was I going to do if that happened?

Questions came fast and furious. What was his diagnosis? Should he be in a locked facility? Was he a danger to himself and others? Should I have called the Psychiatric Emergency Team for them to evaluate him last night? Would he show up to his appointment with Dr. Holden, or would he go to work and have another episode there? What was my responsibility?

I had never been in a situation like this one before. *What was I to do?*

I started using the deep breathing technique I had used with Luke the night before. It was amazing how quickly I was able to calm myself down with it and, once calm, I knew I could wait to see what Dr. Holden said after she saw him.

She had texted me that we'd talk soon after she evaluated him. It was in her hands now. There was a part of me that hoped she'd decide he needed to be hospitalized and I'd be out of the loop, but there was another part of me who really cared about him and wanted him to be able to work through these murder traumas and be able to live a normal life.

***

I had just finished my shower and was on my second cup of coffee when Dr. Holden called me. She had seen Luke and was prepared to give me her insights.

"MJ, he seems stable now and was able to talk about his fears last night. I believe he just had a panic attack. I have ordered him some Ativan for anxiety and told him to take one when he felt one of these anxiety attacks coming."

I listened to her, but couldn't compute what she was saying. What I had witnessed the night before was not just a panic attack. There was something far more intense and troubling.

"Dr. Holden, I think there was something more than a panic attack going on. You weren't here. You didn't see him. He was a totally different person. He scared me. He was terrified of Aaron. That's what set him off, the fact that Aaron had called him and asked him to go out for dinner. He also told me he felt disconnected from his body and was seeing distortions in his house . When he got to my office he was looking around like he didn't know where he was."

Dr. Holden didn't say anything so I remained quiet.

All I could think about was the possibility that Luke had murdered all of those people, but the thought terrified me and I didn't know how to talk to Dr. Holden about it without her thinking that I was crazy.

Finally, I heard her murmur something into the phone.

"What did you say, Dr. Holden? I couldn't hear you."

"Nothing, I was talking to myself."

I hesitated for a moment before I finally said, "What if Luke killed his family and then his roommates?"

Just uttering those words felt like ice was flowing through my veins and I had a sense of unreality. It felt like I shouldn't be revealing these horrible thoughts about Luke being the murderer.

What was happening to me? I didn't understand why I was so terrified. Was I feeling what Luke was feeling the night before?

"MJ, let's not jump to any conclusions okay? There's no reason to think he was the one who killed those people. It's more likely he's finally connecting his emotions with the reality of what's happened and he can't integrate it yet. So there will be distortions in his thinking and even in the way he sees his surroundings.

"I don't want to see him anymore," I blurted.

"I can understand your concerns, MJ, but I think it would be a mistake to take you off his case at this important time. He's just starting to make some inroads here. He trusts you. You're the one he went to last night when the emotions broke through. You're the one who got him to calm down. You're the one he trusts.

Chapter 43

After getting off the phone with Dr. Holden, I made an appointment with my trauma therapist for the next day. If I was going to continue to see Luke, I needed all the help I could get.

I couldn't deny he scared me the night before, but as the day wore on, I started to see it more clearly and had to agree with Dr. Holden. Luke was probably just starting to open up to the trauma of the murders, both his family's and his roommates', and it came out in distorted thinking and hallucinations.

I was trained to look deeper into how a person reacts, what they say, and how they feel as metaphors into their inner psychic world. If I were to do that with what Luke had experienced the night before, I had to figure out what his reactions were telling me.

For one, Aaron scared him.

Two, he found solace in his bedroom closet.

Three, he separated his body from his mind, and he saw things around him as distortions of what was actually there.

So again, why was Luke so intent on snubbing Aaron? What had Aaron really done to him, or not done? Aaron pressuring to come over to Luke's place triggered Luke's surreal episode. Someone was not telling the truth here and I felt it was the key to this entire mystery.

Luke didn't seem to have any problems with Aaron coming to his therapy sessions with him, but when Aaron called and asked to come over to his home where it would just be the two of them, Luke got scared. I know Luke denied that Aaron had hurt him, but did Aaron say something to him, accuse him, making him feel unsafe alone with him?

There had to be something deeper going on there. Luke's distorted reaction seemed to be genuine and he didn't seem to have any control over it. He didn't have any explanation of why he was so fearful of Aaron. Maybe he didn't really know why he feared Aaron. Maybe Aaron was symbolic for someone or something else.

It was driving me crazy being up against this kind of unknown. I liked to be certain about the facts and usually had an idea of what was behind a client's actions and emotions. What I did know was that the murders were the trauma, but I had no idea why Aaron, or his father, would be a trigger for Luke.

Luke told me he hid in his bedroom closet to feel safe. What was the meaning of that? Was it simply that the closet was the most logical hiding place when someone was scared? Luke was a grown, big man who hid in his closet away from a man who was smaller and less physically fit than he was. Had he reverted to a childhood memory or trauma where he had to hide in his closet to feel safe from a real threat back then? He had told me that he came to see me because he felt there was no place to hide. To hide from what?

Since he was a grown man, why didn't he call me or Dr. Holden and talk about his fears. Both of us had given him instructions to call if he came up against something he didn't understand.

But I reminded myself, he actually did try to call me when he was hiding in his closet and when I repeatedly did not answer, eventually he physically came to seek me out because he felt there really was no safe place for him to hide.

That was on me. I should have been available, but was so wrapped up in my own internal thoughts and emotions that I didn't even feel the vibrations of my phone, nor did I check periodically to see if there was some emergency or issue I needed to take care of.

I had been working on trying not to judge myself harshly, but sometimes I deserved it. I really should have felt or heard my phone buzzing while on my walk down Main Street.

All of this started with Aaron calling Luke and asking to come over to Luke's place. Why would Luke fear Aaron?

What was I missing?

***

Instead of sitting in my little apartment worrying and speculating, I decided to go for a walk. As I descended my stairs and entered my backyard, I saw little Joey playing on Aunt Carrie's patio.

I rushed over to the gate and called out to her, "Hey, Joey. What's up?"

She turned toward me as she heard her name and came running over to where I stood. I opened the gate and she hurled herself into my arms. I picked her up and swirled her around and around in a circle as she laughed and giggled.

"Hi you. Whatcha doin'?"

"I playing."

"Oh yeah. What?"

"I hiding from the pink monstas."

"Oh dear, those pink monsters are here again? Where are they? They haven't found you yet, have they?"

She took my hand and led me to one of the patio chairs. Putting her finger to her lips, she shushed me and told me to be quiet, so they wouldn't hear us. She demanded that I hide behind the chair with her so the pink monsters wouldn't find us.

This was better than a walk. I got into the pink monster game, hiding and whispering so they wouldn't hear us until Aunt Carry called for Joey to come in and eat her lunch.

We both stood up and Joey dutifully walked toward the back door to where Aunt Carry was standing. I followed her to the door.

"Hi, MJ. Want some lunch? I have enough for everyone. It's not much, but if you like leftover pasta, you're in luck."

Of course I loved anything Aunt Carry cooked. Even her leftovers were to die for, so I accepted the invitation to lunch. Exactly what the doctor ordered.

I finished helping to clear the lunch remains and hugged Aunt Carrie and Joey good-bye. As I left, I immediately started ruminating about Luke and his relationship with his brother and father.

I couldn't get past the fact that his breakdown was triggered by Aaron calling him and asking to come see him. There was something about Aaron that Luke feared.

I decided at that point to go on my walk as I had originally planned to clear my mind. When I got to the beach,

I took my shoes off and walked toward the water in my bare feet. The sand was cold on my feet, but it felt good.

Sitting at the edge of where the waves lapped up, I gazed out into the ocean as far as I could see and breathed in the ocean salt air. It felt so good and my mind rested.

I watched as a few joggers ran by, one whose big dog ran ahead of him, stick in its mouth. Life on this beach looked calm, peaceful, fun — a contrast to my tangled inner mind.

I must have sat there long enough to doze off a bit; my head jerked as I was about to fall asleep. A large man, who resembled Aaron, came running toward me and I felt a shock of fear. But just as fast, I realized he wasn't running toward me but past me.

My heart racing, I felt the cold water on my bare feet as I saw that the tide was coming in. I quickly backed away, and grabbed my shoes before they got soaked.

The first thought that came to me was *what if Aaron had killed Luke's family and Luke saw him do it? What if he had repressed the entire episode? What if Aaron was keeping tabs on Luke in order to make sure Luke didn't remember?*

That would explain why Luke was scared of Aaron, even if it was an unconscious fear. It would also explain why Aaron was so concerned about Luke and why he kept trying to befriend him and keep close tabs on him.

Chapter 44

When I returned to my apartment, I noticed I had several messages on my phone. I'll admit I'm not very good at keeping my phone with me, and almost always have it turned off. You'd think I would have learned from the night before.

There were four messages from Aaron. They were short and to the point, "Call me. It's important."

He answered on the first ring. His voice sounded strained, "I'm so glad you called. I can't get hold of Luke."

"Aaron, I saw Luke last night. He came to my office and then went and stayed at his friend John's place. He saw Dr. Holden this morning. He's okay."

"Oh my god."

"Aaron, what's going on?"

"I don't know, Dr. Lange. I called him to ask him out for dinner last night and the next thing I knew, he hung up on me and wouldn't answer any of my calls to him after that."

"Aaron, did you say anything to him that might have upset him? Or, did he say anything to you that was worrisome?"

"I just asked him if he'd like to go out for dinner. My treat. I told him I'd come pick him up."

"That's it?"

"Well, after he hung up on me, I got worried and jumped in my car and swung by his place to check to see if he was okay."

"Did you see him? Talk to him in person? Knock on the door? Shout out to him?"

"I didn't see him, but I did knock on his door and shout out to him. All the lights were off, so I thought that he had gone out. I wasn't sure what to do, so I left."

"What made you think that he might be in trouble? Why did you rush over there just because he hung up on you? There must have been something else. After all, I gather he's refused to see you in the past, right?"

We went back and forth, but there didn't seem to be anything Aaron could think of that would have had Luke hang up on him. Or at least that was what Aaron told me.

I also noticed that he didn't really answer my question about why he was so concerned about the night before.

"Aaron, think. There must have been something else. Even if it was something insignificant."

"I pretty much told you what happened, Dr. Lange. Except that once he hung up on me so quickly, I had a weird kind of premonition that something wasn't right."

"What kind of premonition, Aaron? What did you think was going to happen?"

I could feel the muscles in my neck tensing up and consciously tried to relax them.

"I don't really know, Dr. Lange. Just that he was acting so funny. I've asked him out a lot before, and he'd never just hang up on me. He'd either agree to come, or politely decline, claiming he was busy, even though I knew he wasn't. I've grown to just accept that about him, but I keep trying to connect."

***

After we hung up, I felt that familiar feeling in my gut that told me there was something very wrong with this entire scenario. But I didn't really know what it might be. I felt that Aaron wasn't being totally honest with me. He must have said something to Luke, or maybe Luke said something to Aaron that he wasn't admitting to me. After my suspicions about Aaron, I started to see the entire scene from last night very differently.

My head was starting to ache and my shoulders were tense. I laid down on the floor and put my feet up on the sofa in order to try and relax. The anxiety was growing inside of me and I could feel myself rushing toward a panic attack.

I slipped my hand into my pocket to retrieve my cell phone and found soothing music to listen to as I breathed in for count of four, held my breath for four counts, and exhaled for a slow count of eight.

I continued this breathing until the panic receded and the walls stopped closing in on me and I felt like I could get up and breathe normally.

If this wasn't a time to have a shot of vodka, I didn't know what was. There was such chaotic thinking going on in my mind that I couldn't tell what was real and what was just my own fears coming up. I could tell that I was spinning out of control and needed something to ground me so I could think better and get some clarity.

I grabbed my purse and practically ran down the steps to my car. All I could think about was getting that first shot into my stomach, so I could numb all the terror and horror I was trying to keep down.

I wasn't sure if I should go to a bar so I'd be with other people, or grab a bottle and bring it back home.

Drinking alone in my apartment, with Luke and Aaron knowing where I lived, was a scary thought. Was I scared of both of them? Did I think one or the other would hurt me? Or was I scared that I'd find out that one or the other murdered five people? Was this the secret that was being protected?

When I saw a little bar on Main Street, I parked and went in.

It was dark and I could smell the stale beer that had probably been spilled on the floor and saw that there was only one other person sitting at the bar.

It was embarrassing to be in a bar, alone, in the middle of the afternoon, but the need to drink in the company of other people was too strong. It never occurred to me to call Big Al, or my best friend, Franny. All I could think about was to stop the fear that resided in my guts.

I ordered two shots of vodka from the bartender, who swiftly pulled out two shot glasses and filled them up. He didn't say a word and neither did I.

After downing the liquor and feeling that warm, familiar feeling as it hit my stomach, I let out a sigh and then drew in a deep, deep breath.

I looked around the shabby bar and felt safe, but for how long?

Chapter 45

Feeling no pain, I glanced at my watch and wondered where the time had gone. I didn't know how many shots I had consumed and thought that maybe I had blacked out for a bit. I was no longer on the barstool, but sitting at a table with an empty bottle of vodka before me.

I sat up straight and pushed myself away from the table. It felt sticky and disgusting. I was sure I hadn't drunk an entire bottle of vodka by myself and sure enough, I noticed a smelly guy sitting to the left of me.

"Ah, shit."

"Waa?" He was so drunk, he was weaving side to side with that glassy eyed stare of the professional alcoholic.

I was mortified and felt my stomach revolt from drinking hard liquor on an empty stomach. I looked around for a bathroom and barely made it before I threw up in the disgusting dirty toilet, asking myself if this wasn't a low enough point for me yet, then what was?

After splashing my face with cold water, I felt the buzzing of my phone in the pocket of my jeans and tried to extract it before it went to voicemail. I was too late, but I saw the call came from Otto.

In my blurry, drunken state, I had a difficult time remembering who Otto was and when I did, I couldn't fathom why he'd be calling me.

I left the bathroom and promptly ordered a black coffee, strong.

"Girl, you okay?"

It was the bartender looking at me with concern in his eyes.

"Yeah. Just get me a coffee please."

I needed to be somewhat coherent when I called Otto back.

As I sipped on the strong coffee, it reminded me of the terrible coffee at Big Al's AA meeting and all I could feel was remorse and shame. What had I done? It seemed to me that going to the AA meetings was making my drinking worse; not better. I'd never stooped this low before — going to a nasty, hole-in-the-wall bar in the middle of the afternoon, blacking out and getting drunk with a filthy stranger. What was happening to me? And why was Otto calling me?

With that thought, my phone began to buzz again and this time I answered before it went to voicemail. No surprise that it was Otto.

"Dr. Lange? I was trying to call you."

"Yes, I can see that. What's up?"

"What's going on down there?"

"What do you mean?"

"Aaron called and left me a disturbing voice message. He's not answering me back. Have you talked to him lately?"

"I actually did talk to him earlier today about Luke. Why? What did he say?"

I started to feel that fear again. I didn't really want to hear Otto tell me what Aaron said. It would have to be bad if Otto was calling me about it."

"Look, I'm on my way down there. I'll be there in a couple of hours, but do you think you can get hold of Aaron and see if he's okay?"

"Otto, why wouldn't Aaron be okay? What did he say to you?"

"It wasn't so much what he said, but the sound of his voice when he said it. He said that if anything should happen to him, to tell his mother that he loved her very much. Then he told me to keep his memory alive for his son and to apologize to his wife."

Oh dear god, it sounded like a suicide message, but why would he harm himself? He didn't sound suicidal to me earlier in the day. Something must have happened. It had to be something to do with Luke. Was Luke threatening to expose him? Did Luke remember what happened in New Orleans. Had he remembered that it was Aaron who killed his family?

"Otto, did he tell you where he was calling from?"

"No, he did not. Listen to me, Dr. Lange. The thing that got me really worried is the last thing he said."

"What was that?"

"He told me that he was sorry he was such a rotten son and that he loved me."

I wished the coffee could make me stone cold sober, but it didn't. I knew this was something very serious, but I couldn't wrap my alcoholic muddled brain around it.

I took in big gulps of air and drank the remaining coffee and asked for another cup to go.

"Let me try to find Aaron and Luke, okay? Where is Aaron staying, do you know?"

"I already called the Marriott Hotel and they told me that Aaron checked out earlier this mornin'. I have no idea where he might be. I'm very worried about him, Dr. Lange. He hasn't told me he loves me since he was a little boy."

"Okay, Otto, let me think this through. He was trying to get together with Luke last night and had conveyed concern about Luke this morning, so let me find Luke. I'll call you as soon as I know anything."

Chapter 46

"Oh shit, oh shit, oh shit."

I had been trying not to swear. However, this situation seemed to call forth a litany of swearing because I was still drunk and I knew there was something terribly wrong with Aaron and Luke and I felt an urgent need to find them to prevent the disaster that I knew was about to happen.

As I drove over to John's place, thinking that's where Luke should be, I placed a call to Aaron. After getting his voicemail, I called Luke. Same result.

As a last resort I called John. Luke had stayed with him the night before and I thought that maybe John knew where Luke had gone.

"Please answer, please answer."

No answer there either.

Where was everyone?

When I finally got to John's house, I was relieved to see him get out of his car and walk up to his front door.

"John, John, wait up," I yelled at him as I dashed from my car.

"MJ?"

Panting from running over to him, I asked him if Luke was still staying at his house.

"No, Luke left early this morning. He told me he was going back home. He had some chores to do there and thanked me for putting him up again. Why? Is there something wrong?"

I wasn't sure how to answer him, so instead, asked him to let me know if Luke showed up and if so, to keep him there. I ran back to my car and sped away to Luke's house, praying that he'd be there and everything would be all right.

I wasn't sure why I had thought something bad was in the making, because I really didn't have any concrete evidence that Luke or Aaron had done anything bad, or that they would hurt each other. But after hearing Otto's concern, I was becoming more and more convinced that something was terribly wrong.

Since I was still feeling a bit drunk, I carefully slowed down so as not to be picked up for speeding. That internal fear had taken hold and I tried not to hyperventilate.

All I could think about was the possible horror that awaited me at Luke's place. Just like when I found my dad slumped over on his man cave sofa in the garage that horrible night.

I tried not to think about it. I also tried not to think about the night when I was almost killed by the fraudulent detective.

But my guts said that something terrible was about to happen and I needed to be there in order to prevent it.

When I got to Luke's place and parked, I saw that his little house in the back was lit up like a Christmas tree. The front door was open, and as I approached, I heard angry voices from inside. They sounded like Luke and Aaron.

I quickly texted Otto, telling him I was at Luke's place and that his boys were there.

As I entered the open door, I saw the two men facing each other. Luke had a gun pointed at Aaron, who was trying to calm him down.

It was surreal. I had no idea why Luke had a gun pointed at Aaron. I had no idea where Luke even got the gun. I didn't know he even owned one, although I had never asked him.

The energy in the room was like a blazing fire; crackling, popping, sizzling. The bright lights in the room created the illusion of it being daylight and every tiny movement was highlighted by the glare of light.

I entered, then froze — taking in the scene. I could see it was a standoff, beads of sweat started dripping from my forehead as I contemplated what I should or should not say or do.

Luke was the first to notice me and he pointed the gun at me for a nano second and then right back at Aaron.

I was terrified when he pointed the gun at me. When he pointed it back at Aaron, I managed to say, "Luke, what are you doing? It's me Dr. Lange."

"Go away, Dr. Lange. I don't want to hurt you. You don't want to witness this. Go away. I will shoot him."

Aaron was being very still and very quiet, but I could see the look of fear on his face. I felt if I could just keep Luke talking and answering my questions, then maybe I could avert this tragedy.

"Luke, you don't want to do this."

"Yes, I do."

"No, you don't. Why are you holding a gun on Aaron? What happened? Something must have happened. What was it?"

Tears were streaming down Luke's face as he answered, "Ask him. Ask him who killed my family?"

Oh my god! Had I been right? Had Luke seen Aaron kill his family and he was just remembering it now? All the avoidance of Aaron in the past — was it his subconscious mind knowing that it was, in truth, Aaron? And now he was going to get his revenge?

"Tell her Aaron. Tell her the truth. No more lies, no more hiding. TELL HER!"

"Luke, I didn't kill your family. Yes, I was there that night, but I came in after they were already dead. You were standing over them."

"Liar, liar!"

"Luke, Luke. Listen to me," I said. "Did you just remember something about that night?"

His eyes were searching the room and his hands on the gun were shaking so badly, I thought he might shoot it by mistake and accidentally hit one of us. The thought that I should be calling the police entered my mind, but I felt like I didn't dare move for fear that it would scare Luke even more.

"Luke, look at me. It's me, Dr. Lange. Remember, you came to my house last night because you wanted to feel safe. You felt safe there, right? Let's go back there to my house so you can feel safe."

He momentarily looked over at me, but then shook his head as if to clear it and pointed the gun more aggressively at Aaron.

"I remembered. I saw you there that night. You were there. It was you who killed them. I remembered. You're a liar. Tell the truth."

Aaron put his hands higher in the air and said, "Okay, no more lies. I will tell you the truth, but could you stop pointing the gun at me."

When Luke lowered the gun slightly, Aaron continued, his hands up in supplication, "Luke, I came to visit you. I had just learned I had a half-brother and I came to New Orleans to find you. I couldn't wait to meet you, so I had a taxi let me out in front of your house that night. It was dark but your house was lit up with bright lights and I knocked, but no one answered. I went around to the side to see if maybe everyone was out in the back. I saw that a side door was open, so I stepped into what was the kitchen and called out to see if anyone was home."

"Liar!"

"Luke, just answer this one question. Did you actually see me kill them, or did you just see me there?"

Luke furrowed his eyebrows for a second and then, blinked and said, "You're just trying to confuse me. Shut up. Shut up. Let me think."

Aaron continued anyway, "I heard a noise, so I kept calling out and when I went into the living room, I saw you standing over your family with a large knife in your hand. My first thought was that you had killed them."

"What? I came home and found them like that. Today, I remembered seeing you there. You were there that night. I looked up and you were there."

"Luke, I didn't kill your family. I have no idea who killed them, but you were covered in blood and holding the knife looking so lost and devastated. I figured that you had come upon the murders and picked up the knife. You were in shock. I knew I needed to get help for you. I was the one who called the police."

Aaron sounded so compassionate and loving that at that moment, listening to his account of what happened, I realized that Aaron hadn't killed Luke's family, but was relating what he had seen that night. He had seen Luke standing over his family with a knife in his hand.

At that moment, I realized that it was most likely Luke who had killed his family and then years later his roommates. It all started to make sense to me and I knew that Luke was starting to remember what actually happened. If it was Luke, I needed to get him someplace safe to contain the reaction he would have when he remembered all of it, and especially what he'd done.

I stood and watched the drama unfold for a minute when I felt, rather than saw, a presence beside me. It was Otto. I didn't have time to explain it all to him and I hoped that he wouldn't do anything stupid that would cause Luke to shoot. It looked like Luke was actually listening to what Aaron was saying and that we might be able to talk him down, or at least persuade him to give us the gun.

We all held our breath as minutes ticked by and I tried to think of what the right thing would be to say or do. I understood that Luke had to believe that Aaron killed his family, or he wouldn't be able to live with himself. Killing Aaron would somehow bring him some form of justice for the loss of his family. At least, that's what I was thinking at the moment.

I had to somehow keep him from shooting Aaron until we could get the gun from him, so I said, "Luke, I'm going to walk toward Aaron, okay?"

This distracted Luke and he watched me slowly walk toward Aaron, but kept the gun pointed at him. When I got to Aaron, I stood in front of him and looked at Luke and said, "Luke, you don't want to shoot me, right? Please put the gun down."

Some kind of surreal calmness came over me as I stood there looking at Luke, and at that moment, looking down the barrel of his gun, I felt at peace. I gave him a little smile of reassurance, knowing that we had a bond of trust. I hoped that bond would work for him to trust me again and eventually give the gun up.

He returned the smile and at that point, it felt like there was only Luke and me in the room. He slowly lowered his gun and said, "I'll tell you a truth, Dr. Lange. Having my family murdered and being brought out here to California made my life better. It was hell living there with all the dope and alcohol. I hated it. I could never clean up enough to get the smell of the cigarettes and drugs out of the very walls, the cupboards, the drapes, my clothes. I hated it. Cleaning, cleaning, cleaning, never enough food to eat, and living in squalor. It was a terrible way to live. I liked it here.

"But then Sahara and Joy had to come and ruin it all. Smoking, stinking up the place, inviting men over, doing who knows what. Dirty, filthy, drug users. Just like Mama and Auntie Bessie; never cleaning after themselves."

Before I could respond, Otto spoke up, probably guessing that a confession was coming, "Luke, don't say anything more. We're gonna take you somewhere to get you help, okay? Here, Son, give me the gun. You don't need it anymore. We're gonna help you get better." With that, he reached out to Luke for the gun.

Luke looked at Otto as if he had no idea who he was. He looked around like he had done the night before at my place. I knew he was either hallucinating or seeing the room distorted and I could see his agitation and fear start to grow. He was most likely disassociating from reality again after being interrupted by Otto.

Before I could think of what to say, I saw him raise his gun again and point it toward Aaron and me. With lightening speed, I flung my body at Luke as he discharged the gun, causing a deafening explosion near my left ear as the shot rang out.

There was an instantaneous flurry of activity as Otto ran to see if we were hit, and I found myself entangled with Luke on the ground, the gun not more than a few feet away from us.

My focus was on the gun, and since I had lost most of my hearing from the gun being discharged so close to my ears, it created a false sense of our movements happening in slow motion.

Luke and I noticed where the gun was placed at the same time and we both rose together and fought to be the first to take possession of it.

Being bigger and faster, Luke beat me to it and stood up, towering over us, gun in hand. We all froze as he looked at the gun, unsure as to what he should do with it. My heart was beating so fast that I thought it was going to jump right out of my chest, but he didn't point it at any of us.

I realized that he was going to shoot himself. I didn't know how I knew, but I knew. I called out to him saying, "Luke, listen to me. Just listen to me. You trust me right? Don't do it."

I made a move toward him, holding out my hand for the gun. He looked confused and then he smiled his dazzling smile and said, "I'm sorry, Dr. Lange."

As he turned the gun toward himself, I screamed and launched myself at him, but I was too late. He had already put the gun in his mouth and fired.

Aaron ran over to him and futilely attempted to fix the damage, saying, "No, no, no, no," over and over again. Otto walked over and sat down on the floor beside his two sons — one dead, one alive.

He gently grabbed Aaron away from his brother and cradled him in his arms. He tenderly spoke to him, "Son, it's gonna to be all right. It's all gonna to be all right. You'll see. We'll get through this together. Hush now. You're safe."

My whole view of Otto changed at that moment. There was such tenderness and love coming from him toward his two sons that I had to look away.

I used the last of my adrenaline to call the police and when I heard the sirens coming toward the house, I let go and sat down on the floor, closing my eyes against the carnage in front of me.

Chapter 47

Dr. Holden came over to my place to debrief the next day. I wasn't emotionally present and didn't really want to talk. She told me what I expected she'd say: that it wasn't my fault, that Luke had a severe Dissociative Disorder, unable to come to terms with what he had done. She suggested that Luke may have been able to live his entire life having dissociated from the murder of his family if he hadn't been triggered by his roommates.

No matter what Dr. Holden said, I still blamed myself and I knew I would be feeling guilty for a very long time and informed her that I wasn't sure I should continue to work as a psychotherapist. She suggested that I take a break and not make any rash decisions, but it didn't feel rash to me.

Apparently, Aaron had told Dr. Holden that he really didn't think that Luke had killed his family, but felt that Luke may need extra support at some time to deal with the loss and trauma, and that was why he was keeping close tabs. Aaron really did care about Luke and had wanted to help him. He wanted to have a brother.

I saw that Jesse had left me several texts and a few voicemails, but I didn't have the energy to reply. I decided to think about Jesse later.

I slept for days, feeling rather than seeing Aunt Carrie come and go, leaving food for me to eat, and then taking it, untouched, away again. I felt her throw a blanket on me when the evenings turned chilly. I vaguely noticed baked cookies on my counter.

When it was finally time for Luke's funeral, I did manage to take a shower and put on some presentable clothes. Aunt Carrie and Franny came with me and we sat near the back.

It was a short affair and after it was over, we were invited for some refreshments in a different area of the funeral home. There were more people there than I had expected, mostly coming from the warehouse where Luke worked. And the entire Haas family was there, too.

The only good thing I could see that happened with this tragedy was that Aaron and Otto were able to put their differences aside and reconnect. At the funeral, they were still awkward with their affection toward one another, but I could see they were trying, and that made me feel good.

Through my depressed fog, I heard from Aunt Carrie that April and Joey were settling in with her and hopefully were safe from Alex, although the child custody hearing was looming on the horizon.

To be honest, I didn't have a very good feeling about it, but after what happened to Luke, I wasn't feeling very good about much of anything.

I pretended to be fine after the funeral and reassured Aunt Carrie I would be okay and that she should go home and be with her family.

Sitting on my sofa bed, phone in hand, I finally got the courage to call Big Al.

The minute he answered and I heard his voice, I finally broke down and poured my heart out to him.

I admitted to him that I was a fraud, that I lied to myself all the time, that I had gotten drunk instead of helping my client and now he was dead and I was so very ashamed of myself for so many reasons.

When I finally stopped, he said, "Okay, MJ, now we can start."

Read More!

Next up for MJ Lange

"No Witnesses"

The third in the MJ Lange mystery series will be out soon!

Sign up for my newsletter if you would like to be notified when it is available:

https://cindykludtauthor.com/free-prequel

If you haven't read the first book

"No Caller ID"

You can grab a copy at amazon.com

https://www.amazon.com/dp/B0B28D1931

Special Request

Thank You For Reading My Book!

I really appreciate all of your feedback and
I love hearing what you have to say.

I need your input to make the next version of this
book and my future books better.

Please take two minutes now to leave a helpful review
on Amazon where you purchased my book.

Acknowledgments

I wish to acknowledge first and foremost my launch team. You all know who you are. Thank you so very, very much. I appreciate all the time and effort from you.

Developmental editing provided by Edits by Shavonne Clark. Shavonne is making me a better writer and has given me encouragement to keep writing.

My coach at SPS, Ramy Vance, just kept telling me to write. Nothing happens until the book is written.

Without Myles Holar, my Virtual Assistant, nothing would get done because I am a technophobe. She is a godsend.

Finally, I wish to acknowledge all the other creative writers out there, especially in the murder mystery genre for inspiration. I feel a kinship to each and every one of you.

Author Bio

#1 Amazon Best Seller author, Cindy Kludt, uses her experience as a psychotherapist to tell elaborate and chilling tales of her protagonist, psychologist MJ Lange, who inadvertently gets thrown into dangerous situations involving murder.

Growing up without TV, Cindy read murder mysteries as her entertainment and loves authors, such as Mary Higgins Clark who can tell a good story using lovable, flawed, and relatable characters. Her MJ Lange protagonist has been likened to Sue Grafton's, Kinsey Millhone.

Semi-retired and living next door to her energetic six year old granddaughter, Cindy lives 10 minutes from Venice Beach, California which inspires her imagination and colorful characters.

www.ingramcontent.com/pod-product-compliance
Lightning Source LLC
LaVergne TN
LVHW100513110826
845146LV00002B/628

* 9 7 9 8 8 9 1 0 9 0 4 0 8 *